PEOPLE
OF
COVE AND WOODLOT

Stories across
100 years
of
memories

Ted Leighton
&
Alexander Leighton
Illustrations by Eva McCauley

People of Cove and Woodlot: stories across 100 years of memories
© 2025 Frederick Leighton

Cover art and interior illustrations: Eva McCauley
Cover design: Rebekah Wetmore
Editor: Andrew Wetmore

ISBN: 978-1-998149-62-9
First edition March, 2025

Moose House Publications
2475 Perotte Road
Annapolis County, NS B0S 1A0
moosehousepress.com
info@moosehousepress.com

Moose House Publications recognizes the support of the Province of Nova Scotia. We are pleased to work in partnership with the Department of Communities, Culture and Heritage to develop and promote our cultural resources for all Nova Scotians.

We live and work in Mi'kma'ki, the ancestral and unceded territory of the Mi'kmaw people. This territory is covered by the "Treaties of Peace and Friendship" which Mi'kmaw and Wolastoqiyik (Maliseet) people first signed with the British Crown in 1725. The treaties did not deal with surrender of lands and resources but in fact recognized Mi'kmaq and Wolastoqiyik (Maliseet) title and established the rules for what was to be an ongoing relationship between nations. We are all Treaty people.

Production rights

Also by Ted Leighton

The Rick Robichaud novels

A Ring of Justice

Rick Robichaud abandoned science to stay
home and support his wife's career as a veter-
inarian near the village of Bear River, Nova Scotia, where old ways and new, fair play and foul,
generosity and crime weave threads of joy and
hatred, contentment and murder.

  Rick must untangle the threads to reveal
startling truths, uncertain justice and the en-
during power of friendship

Knowers and Lovers

Rick, Zora, and their child, Bronwyn, find themselves in the eye of a storm of events that plays
out in the forests, fields and sea coasts of Digby
County, Nova Scotia; in board rooms in Russia
and situation rooms at NATO; and in piracy on
the high seas. It probes the nature of greed and
hubris, contrasts these with friendship and
mutual care, and gives the last word to Walt
Whitman.

...available from Moose House Publications

Digby County

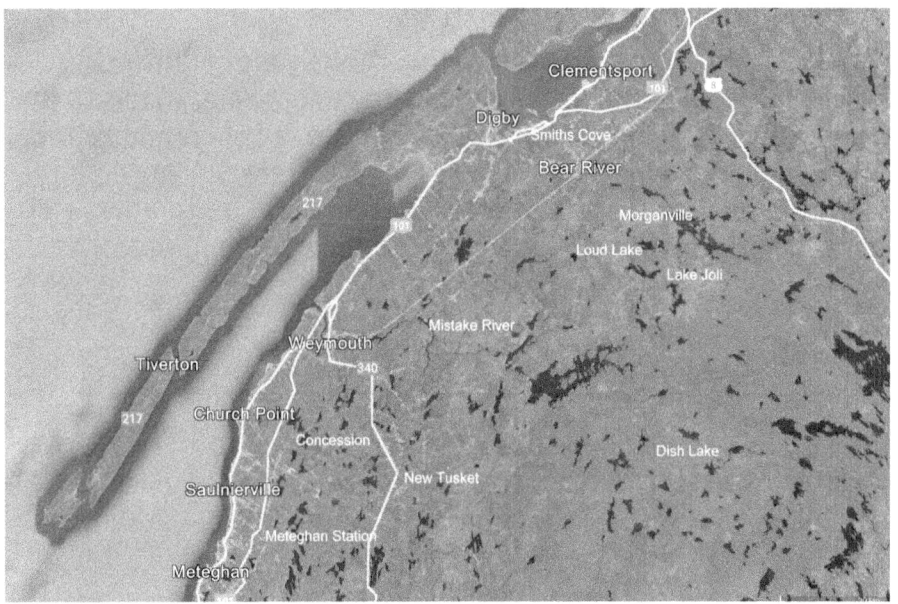

Digby Country

This book is dedicated to **Dorothea Cross Leighton**,
a special friend of the Navajo, Hopi and Zuni peoples in the 1940s,
a pioneer in bringing understanding of diverse beliefs and cultures
into health service programs, co-founder of the Stirling County
Study of mental illness, much-loved member of the Smith Cove's
Society of Friends, sage, mother and grandmother.

People of Cove and Woodlot

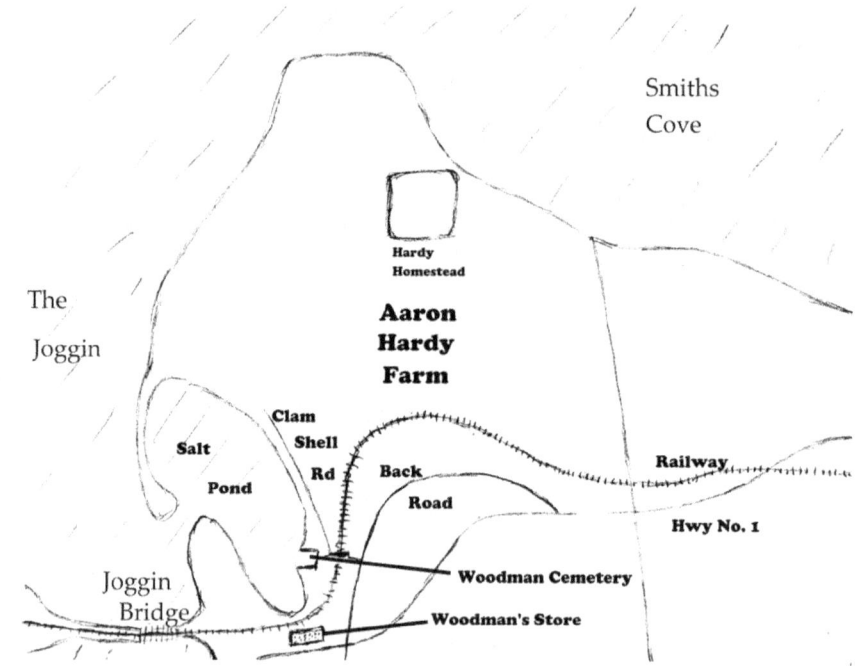

Sketch map from 1960 of Joggin Bridge, including the general area of the Aaron Hardy farm.

A greeting from Alec Leighton

In Digby County, Nova Scotia, the community of Joggin Bridge finally went missing in the 1990s, when Highway 101 and its Exit 25 were built over what remained of it. The small farms and store and houses and railway gradually were worried away by the imperatives of vehicle transportation.

The cemetery that had anchored the settler families to the place for 200 years survived this burial, however, and has remained a place of peaceful beauty, tucked away just off the old Clam Shell Road, overlooking the Salt Pond. You can visit it still, this place of lasting rest with a fine view.

Many of my friends are commemorated in this "Woodman cemetery," as it is known, but I myself am not among them. In 1936, my parents gave my new bride and me an old and abandoned farm located a short distance east and around the shore from Joggin Bridge, on the western shore of Smiths Cove. It was a wedding present then and, eventually, it became my home.

I buried my mother there, and then my father, on an east-facing hill looking out on Bear Island, their passings marked by a granite boulder surrounded by a drystone wall. This is where you will find me now, also, another small glacial erratic marking the beginning and end of my own passage through time.

In my last two decades, my thoughts returned frequently to the landscape and the people of the coves and forests of Atlantic Canada, who, in the 1920s especially, had nurtured me into young adulthood and out into the world, and who, in the 1950s and 60s, did the same for my son, Ted. There is a hybrid vigour here in the mix of cultures and ways of seeing things. On these pages, we have tried to portray some of the people we have best remembered.

Alec Leighton memorial stone.

The Magic Show begins

The Magic Show

It was in the 1950s that I first heard the down-east Maine stories performed by Robert Ryan and Marshall Dodge as the stage characters *Bert and I*, and one line from one of their stories stayed with me. In it, an elderly man is brought before a judge for some misdemeanour and the judge routinely asks the man where he lives.

The man replies, "Down Bailey Island way."

"Have you lived there all your life?"

"Not yet."

This reply seemed to me a fine lesson in optimism and a caution against hasty judgments. "That was the best day of my life!" never can be stated with confidence until one's time on earth truly is over. Now, however, I can speak from the vantage point of my own life's completion to say that my experiences with the "Magic Show," at the age of 21, guided me forever afterwards.

The "Magic Show" was an adventure of a few weeks' duration, concocted by me and two friends, Bill Doerflinger and Danny Mannix. We were college students then, each of us hoping to become a writer of some kind. Bill was a skilled amateur magician and Danny wanted to become one.

So we conspired to tour the back roads of Digby County in the summer of 1929, offering magic shows wherever we could. Bill would preform, accompanied by Danny, and I would sell our small packages of beginner do-it-yourself magic tricks.

Who was I in the summer of 1929? I was the only son of a newly-rich family of Irish immigrants to the United States. That wealth would tumble substantially a few months later, but we remained well-to-do even so.

With an American partner, my father co-founded the construction company Irwin and Leighton soon after he arrived in Philadelphia in 1906. I was born two years later, and I mostly was schooled by private tutors and moved around with my mother as she whimsically might decide to spend several months in Ireland or elsewhere from time to time.

Despite their wealth, my parents were denied the social status in Philadelphia that their financial position otherwise would have assured them. They were Irish, and thus inadmissible. By way of example, Mrs. Irwin, the wife of my father's business partner, insisted that the official papers of incorporation of the new company must state that there would be no social obligations or contact between the two families.

So mine was a childhood of both pride and prejudice, and very limited relationships with people outside of my own family. It also was hugely privileged. I never knew, and seldom saw, material want.

My parents found refuge in Nova Scotia when the First World War made travel back to Ireland impossible and they had sought a summer place away from Philadelphia. From age 8 to 24, I came to know, and became fully bonded to, the landscapes of Digby County, of Digby town, Smiths Cove and Bear River, with long guided camping trips deep into the Acadian forest and much local wandering, mostly by myself. I read widely, studied the essentials of school with tutors, and the family would recite the great poets to each other at dinner.

The "Magic Show" changed forever how I saw humanity and the world. It took me out of my comfortable drawing room, decorated with family portraits and selective understandings, and threw me into the street.

Bud and Bernice Saulnier

In order to give some real-life flavor to the "Magic Show", and to avoid as much as possible it being just a lark for three well-to-do young men, we decided we would support ourselves entirely from what we could earn. We hid a small emergency fund in the depths of our wagon, but we each felt that any use of it would be crossing the line into failure.

On the day we set out from Smiths Cove, the weather was inspirational. I remember our horse and wagon creaked up the whaleback ridge above the Acacia Valley under limitless blue sky, with patches of white cloud making dark shadows dash across the land. On the right, the sea reached toward us through North Mountain to create bays, coves, and tidal rivers. On the left, the forest undulated off across the plateau of South Mountain, hiding in its hollows a multitude of lakes, streams, bear, moose, and solitudes.

At the end of the first day, we arrived at a small settlement clustered about a sawmill on a stream called Mistake River. The settlement is gone now, but on that evening the road was alive with men, women and children, and they gathered around us as soon as our wagon pulled up.

We arrived tired, hungry and despondent at not having sold a single magic package all day. The name "Mistake River" seemed full of ill-omen.

However, the little crowd around us inspired our magician Bill to stand up on the back of the wagon and start producing illusions. As the audience gasped, gee-whizzed and stretched its eyes, Bill was roused to give a show that lasted nearly an hour. Dan assisted him with elegant gestures while I held the horse to keep her from running away when people laughed and cheered.

Our own eyes soon were stretched as well. Half-way along in the show, Bill came to a trick that required him to borrow a quarter from someone in the audience. The request seemed to freeze them.

Picking out by means of eye contact a plump and happy-looking woman who must surely be rich enough to have a quarter, Bill put the question directly to her. She giggled and shook her head.

Then a man spoke up. "Bernice, give him a quarter.

"I ain't got none."

"You ain't got none? What you done with that 50 cents I give you the week before last?"

Nobody laughed. This was not a joke.

The man who spoke, Bud Saulnier, was one who had attracted our attention from the beginning of the show, and he had taken a bit of getting used to, especially on Bill's part. This was because, although he was a tremendous enthusiast for the magic and at the conclusion of every trick uttered cries of appreciation, his expressive vocabulary was limited to a few words of blasphemy and swearing:

"I'll be dammed!"
"I'll be God Jeesily dammed!"
"Look at that fool! Christ in a bucket!"
"How did the bloody sucker do that? Well if he ain't a fool!"
"Now look what the stinkin' thing done."

and so on. It seemed to me, whose mother recited Shelley at dinner and requested Keats in return, that this man must know very few words for positive strong feeling, a limitation it seemed to me, like forever wearing a muzzle. Was it from a lack of education? It was a bit dizzying to think about how he might go about making love. To me, this was a new and somewhat frightening way of being.

After the show, though, it was this same Bud Saulnier and his wife, Bernice, who took us into their home, in which twenty-five cents was meant to serve as spending money for two weeks.

They gave our horse a stable for the night and invited the three of us into the shelter of their small and thin-walled house with its two rooms downstairs and a loft overhead, reached by a ladder nailed to one wall. They could not have afforded to offer three hungry young men a meal, but they urged us to use their kitchen stove to prepare our own food and to eat at their table.

As we did so, the community's children flooded into the house to watch us. As most of this crowd finally ebbed away, five children remained, whom we presumed to be Bud's and Bernice's own.

In the course of the evening, we learned that Bud could not read, but was tremendously proud that his wife could. He made her demonstrate.

He also showed us a magic trick of his own. He could smoke a cigarette inside out, with the lighted end in his mouth and the butt protruding. He could smoke about half a cigarette that way, shooting out clouds of smoke through his nose and the corners of his mouth.

We were offered the loft for the night. There were no beds, but it was pleasant nevertheless. We spread our blankets on the floor boards and dropped off to sleep listening to the sounds of the flowing river.

I was awakened in the morning by Bud down below talking to his youngest child, a girl perhaps one year old. The words came up to us in loving tones, like the morning sunlight coming in through the cracks in the walls.

"Where's that little nose? *There* it is! Where's them little eyes? *There* they are! Where's that little smile? *There* it is!"

That monologue still flows as a melody through my memory, like the Mistake River itself. I had just heard loving poetry from the heart of a man far beyond the reach of Shelley and Keats. It was a stark encounter for me with the haughty contempt through which I had viewed people like Bernice and Bud Saulnier, and a first stab into my own heart of some much-needed humility.

Innocent Comeau

Don't depend on selling them there little packages.
Charge admission.
You'll make a lot more money.

These words of advice were offered by a man just introduced to us: Innocent Comeau. We had given an impromptu show at Marie Gaudet's restaurant near L'Anse des Leblancs, in appreciation for her generosity in taking us in and giving us beds for the night. Innocent had been in the audience. He had liked the show and wanted us to come to his store in Concession the next day and perform there. The store had a hall upstairs, and we could have it without charge.

What could we do, but thankfully agree? We promised to be in Concession by six the next evening, for a show at eight.

We followed Innocent Comeau's advice and charged admission right up front: twenty-five cents for adults, ten cents for children; babes in arms were free.

There was no electricity in Concession in those days, and we performed in the warm, yellow glow of lamplight. The show was popular and a real money-maker for us, but what I recall most vividly about that night is Innocent himself, sitting in the front row, surrounded by children of assorted sizes, with a few of the smaller ones on his knees, leading the laughter proudly and happily.

That night, we were welcomed into Innocent's home, which was a short distance from the store, near the edge of a lake. It was a large house, with several generations living together and lots of children.

The household and younger children were managed, loved and cared for by Saraphie Cromwell from Southville, east of Weymouth, who had been employed by Innocent ten years previously, when his wife, Rosie, and their newborn daughter died in the influenza pandemic of 1918. Altogether, Innocent and Rosie had 16 children.

The next morning, before daylight, we were awakened by great stirrings throughout the house, and by six o'clock we were gathered around a breakfast from Saraphie's kitchen that began with half of a large blueberry pie for each of us. Then came porridge, eggs, bacon, toast, sausage, and pancakes: a bounty aimed at the day of hard labour for everyone that would follow.

Over that unforgettable breakfast, Innocent told us about his life and work. I was mesmerized; I never had met a person like this before. He could plow, harrow, sow, harvest, raise livestock and do all the mechanical, blacksmithing, horticultural and veterinary work necessary for these activities. He could go into the woods in the winter to run a trap line or to fell trees, haul out the logs, and saw them into lumber in his own saw mill. He could build a house with these materials and not only do the carpentry, but also the foundation and chimney masonry and the plumbing. He could equally well go down to the shore of St. Mary's Bay and build a four-masted schooner, launch her, and, with a cargo of his own lumber and a crew of family and neighbours, sail it across the Atlantic to Bordeaux, France. He could then drop down the coast to the easterly trade winds off North Africa and arrive in the Caribbean, where he would take on rum in Cuba and salt at Turks Islands and sail back to Nova Scotia.

And this was not all. He could farm foxes for fur or run a store, as opportunities might present themselves, and he frequently had

Launch of the 'Charlotte Comeau', built by Innocent Comeau, 1919.

shifted his work among business activities according to his assessment of the drift of things. Sailing ships had become a dead enterprise and lumber was in decline. However, markets had developed in eastern cities for blueberries, and there were extensive barrens of wild blueberries of good quality in Western Nova Scotia. So, wild blueberries now were the thing. He and his sons were driving about the countryside in their trucks, exhorting pickers, buying wholesale and bringing the crates to Yarmouth for export to the "Boston States".

Energy, zest, resourcefulness and imagination: this is how I remember Innocent Comeau, a *bricoleur suprème*, a proud yeoman surrounded by stalwart sons, self-taught and self-propelled.

After breakfast, while we sat about stuffed like pythons and trying to digest enough that we could move once again, several of the Comeau boys showed us how they could dance the Juba. They clapped and battered the floor while Innocent played an accordion for them with the same offhand competence he seemed to have in driving a truck, felling a tree, building a ship, or milking a cow.

Faces of Poverty

As we travelled the back roads, we passed through a countryside dominated by poverty, with thin soil, abundant rocks, unpainted houses and children with ragged clothes and bare feet. Yet, on occasion, when telling a ragged child that the fee to attend the magic show was ten cents, I was handed a five dollar bill, a small fortune for that time and place, and asked if I minded changing it. It seemed a magic trick more miraculous than the best of Bill's illusions.

There came an afternoon when we stopped at a farm house along a dusty back road to check our bearings, and were invited down into a root cellar for some heavenly long drafts of cool cider. We were half way through a long day of driving in the hot summer sun, and the visit to the cellar was a deliriously happy interlude. Our host also seemed pleased to have a break from the sun, and he prolonged our visit by explaining to us some aspects of the local economy.

Prohibition in the United States was bringing the area some very welcome prosperity. Men from many local Acadian families had found employment running alcohol from the French islands of St. Pierre and Miquelon, off Newfoundland, to buyers in boats off the coast of New England, and they were making stacks of money, a good, steady, daily wage plus an extra $100 every time a delivery was made.

Some special knowledge and practices were required in this

work. Correct identification of the waiting buyer 12 miles off the American shore was important so that you didn't deliver your cargo mistakenly to a rival gang or to a disguised U.S. Coast Guard boat. The critical element in this case was a precisely-torn American one-dollar bill. When, in the dark of night, a buyer boat came up alongside a Canadian supply boat seeking its illicit cargo, the skipper of the buyer would offer the Canadian skipper half of a torn dollar bill and it had to match the other half, which the Canadian skipper had taken along with the load of booze. If not, there were curses and prompt castings off, and sometimes shots were exchanged. We got the idea that our host himself was a participant in this business and right now was on a home visit between trips.

This new influx of money might have explained some of those five-dollar bills offered for a ten-cent admission, but in other conversations along the way, we learned more. For example:

> This country around here looks poor because it is poor. That is the first thing. It does not have any decent farm land from one end to the other. There is enough woods and off-shore fishing to support some of the people, but not everyone. To get money, you have to have a skill you can sell, and you are better off if you have two or three of them so you can change about with the seasons and the market opportunities.
>
> You keep your house and family here on unmortgaged family property and you have a garden and a cow for some of your food, but a lot of the year you are away working somewhere else. That's where you make the piasters to send or bring back. Or else you set up in something that doesn't call for good land, but takes a lot of family backup in pooled money and helping hands, like a store, a sawmill, a boat yard, or a fox farm.

And also:

> Now, about this unpainted look, there's reasons beyond just being poor. That's some of it, but the older Acadians were like the Scotch; they had very saving natures. On top of that, they learned early on that if you improved the appearance of your property, it put your taxes up. They didn't trust banks neither, too easy for governments to peek in there. So, there's lots of money hidden around some of those unpainted houses.

Toward the end of our magic tour, we arrived in the settlements around Meteghan Station, the railway stop of the Dominion Atlantic Railway serving the whole Meteghan region, two miles inland from the sea. It is a hilly place, with the sound of a river rushing over falls and rocks always audible when you paused to listen.

The centre of activity was a large, water-driven sawmill, together with a company store, the manger of which we soon met because he was chairman of the school trustees and thus the person to ask to use the school for a show.

I cannot now recall this man's face or name, but I remember well what he said to us during our visit. He was very friendly to us, interested in what we were doing and offered us the keys of the school.

We were surprised, then, when he also told us that he would not be coming to our show. He was at pains to assure us that this was not in any way due to any objection he had to the show itself, but that, on principle, he and his family never mixed socially with "the French".

Chatting across the counter of his store, he told us that he was a Protestant from another part of the county and that he spoke no French. He had lived among the Acadians for many years, had made his living from their labour, and had a real fondness for them. He mentioned their honesty, energy and dependability, but he also was a little sad about their "superstitious" beliefs, and about how their priests exploited them unmercifully. He also thought their morals were lax, that they drank too much and that the woods all around were full of illicit stills where they made "Panther Piss (*aka* "panther oui-oui"). His main point was that the French were "not the same as us," so keeping aloof from them was best.

This encounter with such harsh and living tribalism left me sad and despondent. It was a tiny flicker of the same human intolerance that filled the history books with events like the St. Bartholomew's Day massacre, the deportation of the entire population of Acadians from their homelands and "The Troubles" in Ireland, from which I myself once had taken refuge under a bed as stray bullets struck the walls. I feared I was seeing the shadow of the gunman again now, even here in the green glens of Meteghan Station.

Bats and Illusions

Most nights, we camped not far from the side of whatever road we were travelling. We had met our self-imposed test of earning enough to meet our expenses and we had ample groceries.

Since I was neither magician nor majestic assistant, setting up camp, cooking and caring for the horse were the jobs that fell to me. One night, we camped near the opening of a small, abandoned mine of some kind, and, while I prepared an evening meal, Bill and Danny went to explore what they could of the entry tunnel.

I was busily gathering and breaking up small fallen branches to keep the potatoes boiling when Danny burst into camp with an excited declaration.

"Alec, you should have seen it! As I went into the tunnel, a thousand bats flew out and knocked me down!"

Danny and I shared a keen interest in nature and animals, and I dropped everything to run back to the mine with him and see the marvel of those bats if I could.

However, Bill was only a few steps behind Danny in returning to camp and he interjected, "Danny, tell Alec what really happened."

"Well," said Danny, "there were a lot of bats, maybe not quite a thousand. They startled me and I fell over backwards."

"Come on Danny, tell him what *really* happened."

"Well, okay, there were only a few bats and, as they flew past, I tripped on something in the tunnel entrance and fell down."

Bill, with a sigh: "Danny, tell him what *really* happened."

"Well, dammit, there was only one bat. I didn't see it, but Bill saw it and told me about it."

Danny always preferred a good story.

One thousand bats flew out and knocked me down.

As we moved from community to community, giving show after show to the obvious delight of the people attending, I began to wonder what it was about the show that people liked so much. Bill's masterful conjuring, the novelty of a traveling show, and the general party atmosphere our arrival in a community seemed to inspire all had something to do with it. But it became ever clearer to me that the illusions themselves were the greatest appeal.

The people understood full well that it was all trickery and misdirection. A magic trick was successful only in so far as it fooled them. Outsmarting the magician by guessing how he did it also was part of the fun. But as each show went along, people became less and less interested in detecting how the tricks were done, and more captured by some other pleasure that welled up in them as they watched. Many appeared to enjoy pretending that the tricks were indeed real magic, and this often progressed to partly believing that they were, and wanting to believe in them even more completely.

Is there such a thing as an inborn appetite for illusion? Do we all have it? How far can it go? There were times when I was frightened by the credulity of the audience, by their evident desire to believe in something that, by all the general rules of evidence that they themselves applied and lived by every day, they knew to be untrue. I wondered if this might be the shadow of the gunman yet again, a wolf in sheep's clothing.

Most of the settlements through which we passed inland, along the forest edge, had been established a half century before, around lumbering operations and building the railroad. But some of those farthest from the coast, in the deepest forest, were built more recently as part of a mass panic to escape "The Antichrist."

A rumor that "The Antichrist" very soon would appear on earth, would rise out of the sea and destroy all true Christians, had become widely believed in the area a few decades previously, and whole communities had fled to the forest and built secluded dwellings in the hope of escaping this certain calamity.

Those who explained to us this recent origin of their communities could not give us a clear sense of what "The Antichrist" was believed to be. It was in the Bible somewhere and was the Devil seeking to destroy Christians before the second coming of Christ himself, or something like that. Whatever the details, the end of the world was thought to be at hand. Some believers prepared themselves to face the calamity where they lived, while others fled.

After the panic subsided, some participants returned to their former coastal communities while others remained at the inland settlements through which we now were passing, giving our magic show to their descendants. I was hugely affected by this recent history of public panic, set off by a rumour and uprooting whole communities. Thinking about it and trying to make sense of it launched me on a decades-long quest better to understand what relationships there might be among illusion, delusion and hallucination.

New Tusket

Our next-to-last show was given in New Tusket, an English-speaking settlement, mostly of Baptists, 12 miles straight inland from the shore of St. Mary's Bay, deep in the forest. We sought out the chairman of the local school trustees, a Mr. Sabean, and immediately were welcomed into the Sabean family's home and offered the use of the Community Hall.

Like the Saulniers, the Gaudets and the Comeaus, the Sabeans were extremely kind to us. They would not hear of our sleeping in their barn or camping in one of their fields. We were brought into their home and treated like members of their family.

Mr. and Mrs. Sabean were a pair of very strong, like-minded people, busy operating their farm and woodlots and guiding the community of New Tusket. In my memory, Marie Gaudet clearly was the leader in her household and Innocent Comeau was in his, but the Sabeans I remember as co-equal, exerting collaborative formal and informal leadership in church and community, each within his and her traditional role as husband or wife.

The Sabean living room was small but busy because it contained both the post office and the telephone exchange. One of the daughters was the telephone operator. People also came to seek or give advice on matters as varied as potato blight, the best stitch to use in making some part of a dress, what to do for a baby's cough, and how to plan a wedding. They also helped the telephone operator.

"Does anyone here know where Bill Moody is today?" the operator would ask the room.

"Listen, everybody, I've got some sad news. Just heard Johnnie tell Bob that his mom has passed away. The funeral will be tomorrow at two."

"Maggie, on your way home, would you stop in at Katie's and tell her that Purley is trying to get hold of Arthur?"

"There is no use in ringing him, Annie. You know where he is, and she won't answer the phone neither."

At meal times, the Sabeans often discussed some less-public issues that were brought to them as community leaders, such as how to deal with some of the more troubling aspects of their minister's personality, and whether the time had come to see if Dr. Pothier would certify a neighbor as mentally incompetent so they could get her baby away from her before she starved it to death.

One morning, we were witness to what turned out to be an informal trial. The group that assembled in the Sabeans' home included, in addition to Mr. and Mrs. Sabean, several character witnesses, some elders of the community and the accused, who himself would have looked like one of the elders except that he had completely fallen to pieces. The issue to be decided was whether the accused should be turned over to the police or dealt with by the community.

The first part of the proceedings focused on just what the accused had done, which was to feel with his hand between the legs of a mentally-handicapped twelve-year-old girl. For us, it was exceedingly painful to see and hear the accused elderly man's quavering admissions coming out of the ghost of his shattered former dignity.

After considerable talk, a consensus gradually emerged. The action of the accused was wrong and unacceptable, but also seemed to be an anomaly, a lapse on the part of an old man who, otherwise, had a record only of good behaviour during his lifetime in the com-

munity. This lapse might be the result of developing senility. A re-
petition of the same act or the commission of another could be
prevented by watchfulness on the part of his family and friends,
who had declared themselves ready to undertake this responsibility. So far as punishment was concerned, this meeting itself was
punishment enough.

The upshot, therefore, was a kind of suspended sentence with a
warning that, should anything of this sort happen again, authorit-
ies would be notified.

As I reflect on it now, this community decision could be seen as
a kangaroo court and coverup of a crime, but it seems to me that
the kangaroo had displayed an impressive level of balanced judg-
ment and humane feeling for the accused and also for the victim-
ized child who, it was clear from the trial, was loved and protected
within the community and might suffer much as a witness if the
matter went to the courts.

We gave our show of illusions and moved on, but New Tusket
had given us something new and, to me, deeply valuable. As we
travelled our show through Digby County, we had been meeting
people mostly one by one, a living portrait gallery of individuals
each of whom had left their mark on us. In New Tusket, from the
observation post of the Sabeans' living room, we had experienced
first-hand a whole complex, interacting community, and we had
seen how it was very much more than just a sum of its parts.

Onward

We returned from our "Magic Show" adventure elated, trailing clouds of glory. We gave one final performance at a fair for the benefit of the Digby General Hospital, shook hands, and it was over.

In the end, we all did become writers of one kind or another. Bill (William M. Doerflinger) became well-known for his folk-song collections such as *Shantymen and Shantyboys,* which he began the evening we spent in Marie Gaudet's restaurant. He collected and brought to public attention songs that now are widely known, such as *The Leaving of Liverpool* and (*Bound for) South Australia*, and he had a long career in book publishing.

Danny (Daniel P. Mannix, IV) became a carnival magician and sword-swallower (as *The Great Zadma*), and author of many books on a wide range of subjects.

I became a student of people and their mental health, and I studied and wrote about this for 60 years. The "Magic Show" launched us all into the rest of our lives.

Bob Cossett

For as long as I can remember, Robert Burns (Bob) Cossett lived on the beach on the western side of Smiths Cove in a cottage he'd built for himself on a foundation of sturdy driftwood logs. The cottage was at the northeast corner of what once had been the Aaron Hardy farm. Its windows looked north across the Annapolis Basin to Victoria Beach, with its green navigation light flashing at night, and to the majestic ebb and flow of the tides.

Bob and my father were friends. They often rowed out together to fish for flounder. Bob slowly had restored for me the old and broken Hardy family home, and we became his newest and nearest neighbours when my family and I came to live there in the 1940s, after World War II. Bob was a custodian of the history of the place where he lived. He died in 1951, at the age of 79.

In 1946, I asked him if he would tell me all he could about the place where we now lived side by side, and especially about the Hardy family who had farmed this land until the economy had turned against them. He agreed, and on April 26th, a Friday morning, he invited me to his cottage for a first lesson.

He wanted me to write down what he said, word for word as he spoke them, and I tried my best to do so. He paused frequently to ensure that my writing was keeping up with him.

He started the lesson with the history of the Hardy house he had so recently rebuilt.

The house was built before my day. Aaron Hardy built the house, him and his sons. Squire Ned Potter up in Smiths Cove done the carpentry work for forty cents a day, that was his wages. The house would be...Squire Ned Potter...the house is something over a hundred years old, but I can't tell you how much.

Aaron Hardy immigrated to this country from Germany. He was a thoroughbred German. He came out here seeking a homestead. I think he came from a part of Germany up next to Holland. Whether he got his wife here or brought her with him, I can't tell you. But his family—let me count up Aaron Hardy's family—there was one, two, three, four girls and one, two boys, is all I know.

Now there is one or two of the girls that I can't give you their names, but the boys I can. The first, the oldest, was Benjamin, the one who later on owned the place. The next one was Jacob. That is the two boys. Now the girls—which one was the oldest? Oh, what was their names? One was Isaiah Wilson's mother, and one was Deacon Sam Rice's wife. Another one, she married Jabe Snow. That was my wife's mother; that was Elmy Anne.

That was Aaron Hardy's family.

Now, Benjamin Hardy's family, I can give you that. Ben Hardy was married twice. With his first wife, he had Burton and George Henry, and James Irwin, too, but he died young. Then his wife died, and he married Celia Wilson of Marshalltown, Digby County.

For boys, they had Charlie and Forman. The oldest girl was Sarah, and she married Isaac Nelson. She died only a few years ago, at the age of 77 or 78. The next girl to her was Lilian Jerooshy. We always called her Jerooshy but she wrote her name Lilian. There was another girl, her name was Hattie. She died young, at 18, of TB.

That's the record of the Ben Hardy family and they're all dead. No, there's one living yet, Forman is a-living yet, in Bear River, about 80. Ben's brother, Jacob Hardy, had no family that I know of.

Now, the Hardys lived on and owned this property here, yours and mine. It measured 200 acres, from the shore back, a mile and a quarter long. Then, at Aaron Hardy's death, his will divided up the estate.

Now, I can't always remember these girls' names, but I know who they married. Elmy Anne had a lot 16 rods wide and the length of the whole place, a mile and a quarter, that was her share [~40 acres]. Then George Henry, next to her, had 50 acres more, which is my place here. Now Jacob Hardy bought the place next to it, 50 or 75 acres, I don't know which. He was an old drunken article. His share of the homestead was the extension to the Jabe Snow place, from the top of the bank down to low water. That went clear down to the end of the point that is your place now. You'll find deeds to all this I'm telling you about.

When the Aaron Hardy place come to be divided up, it left Benjamin Hardy without no road to get down on the shore at all. The old family road come down to Elmy Anne's place but not to his. So he bought the eight-rod strip of land from Jacob and that took him down far enough to put in a team road down to the beach. You know where it is, all grown to rack now. Benjamin Hardy made that road himself after the place was all divided up.

Ben Hardy's been dead now 44 or 46 years. He deeded everything to Charlie, his son by Cecilia Wilson, the whole place and everything he had. Charlie lived just one year after Benjamin died and then he died without a will, so the property fell back to his heirs.

The next comer was Isaac Nelson, his wife, Sarah Hardy, being senior heir to her brother Charlie's estate. Isaac Nelson was New Brunswick born and American naturalized. They come, him and her, and took charge of the property. Her mother, Cecilia, was still a-living when Sarah and Ike took charge, and Sarah took the responsibility for her mother along with the place.

Ike Nelson bought out five of the other heirs' shares. His wife Sarah's was the sixth share, and there were three more. When the mother Cecilia died, Sarah claimed her share too, but her sisters living at the time wouldn't sign off on that and there were two sub-heirs wouldn't sign off.

One sister died still holding on to her right and one sub-heir died holding on to his. One of the sub-heirs is living yet: Jimmy Evans Hardy in Boston, works for a lumber concern there. But none of the heirs now is no good, they're all out of date.

Well, Ike Nelson run the place in quite a lot, unpaid taxes and all that. Then he died and the place was sold at auction for taxes and expenses. Ralph Cossett here in the Cove bid on it, on behalf of your dad, Archie Leighton. He bought the place at auction for $750. Your family owns it and got a deed for it.

I wanted to know what connections the place had with Isaiah Wilson, Digby County's remarkable historian. I had a life-long fascination with this unusual man. As a child, I would see him walking the roads of Smiths Cove, with a limp and a cane and an aura of living in some inner world. He was a dirt-poor, handicapped almanac-salesman, but he had managed to write a 400 page history of the whole of Digby County up to his own time, limping his way on foot all over the county itself and also several times the 150 miles to the provincial archives in Halifax. Bob had mentioned that Isaiah's Wilson's mother was a daughter of Aaron Hardy. I asked him to tell me about her.

> She was a cousin to all these Hardys, a daughter to Aaron Hardy. She was a queer sort of article. She was indeficient.
>
> Isaiah's mother was Benjamin Hardy's sister. Another of his sisters married Laif Snow and was Oscar, Will and Charlie's mother. Laif is the one that died in the asylum. I think I'm right in that one, but I'd leave a loophole there for a mistake. Laif was in the asylum in Halifax for most of his life, and when they got the poor house fixed in Marshall-town, they took him down there. He lived there all the rest of his life and died there.
>
> That's the other big settler family on this land, the Snows. Jim Snow—I'm pretty sure his name was Jim—Jim Snow come from Germany. The Aaron Hardy family and old Jim Snow were relations by marriage before they left Germany. They both come out here together. They come to New York, and in America, as the feller says, they found no rest for the soles of their feet there, and they came on to Montreal.
>
> They tarried, farming there for awhile, then something happened and they gathered up their families and whole kit, and come to Nova Scotia. Aaron Hardy, when he settled, bought this 200-acre farm, but I do not know who he bought it from. Jim Snow, he bought a homestead up in the Cove, up to where Will Snow lives.
>
> Jim Snow married his wife here. What was her name? She was a Winchester. They had Jabe and Warren and Laif and William, four boys. They had only one girl, Ratia. One of the boys, William Snow, was drowned in Digby Gut with Burton

Hardy, going out a-fishing right here from this creek beside the house.

The eldest son, Jabe Snow, married Elmy Anne Hardy. They had five girls, no boys. The girls' names was...Ida was the oldest one; Jean, that's Eugenia; Alice, well, Belle comes in before that; and there was Edith May, who was my wife. That makes Jabe Snow's family.

Now, Jabe's brother, Laif Snow, married another one of Aaron Hardy's daughters. They had three boys only: Charlie, Will and Oscar. That is Laif Snow's family.

When Oscar was a baby, Laif went crazy, went melancholy first and then went raving. That is the way all the Snows went. Billy Snow, later on, he went the same way.

Now, there was Jim Snow's son, Warren. He had two boys and a girl. His oldest boy's name was Maynard and the younger was Alfred. The girl's name was Thelma, I think. I always knew her well. I think that was her name: Thelma, yeah. Well, that was Warren Snow's family.

Warren Snow's wife died when his youngest, Thelma, was very small, and he brought them up himself. His wife was from Campobello, and she was quite inedeficient in her mind. Warren's mother, who also was Laif's mother and Jim Snow's wife, was crazy, too, had to keep her locked up and she died crazy. Warren had crazy spells himself, but he didn't have to be locked up because he was so harmless, an awful nice fellow.

Yes, Warren's mother run me out of the house many's the time—crazy.

Now, the next generation that would come on would be Laif Snow's sons, Charlie and Oscar and Will. Charlie was educated and became a Baptist minister under United States law. Will's business was as a Bible agent, a sort of evangelist agent for the Bible Society for years and years. Oscar went away to the States, too, when he was young, went into a shoe factory. They all had good education, you know.

Oscar worked up to be a bookkeeper in charge of the factory packing room and all this. He married over in the States, an Irish woman. She had seven young ones by Oscar. The oldest boy's name was Joe. The oldest girl was Madelene. The next boy's name was Billy. The next girl's name was—I don't know what. She was put in the asylum when she was twelve and is there yet. And Billy is there too.

There is one girl a-living on her own brains and sense. She was down last summer and plans on coming down next to look after her property.

Charlie Snow, the Baptist minister, never had a family, and his story is too wild for a minister to carry, so we won't put it down.

Bob's chronicle ended there for that day. His mind was wearied from all the detailed recall. His formal account of local history was not finished, and he would continue it another day.

That day never came, however.

Bob and I chatted a while after his formal recitation, and I learned that the 'crazy' Miss Winchester who married Jim Snow was not related to the Winchesters I myself knew around Smiths Cove and Joggin Bridge, and that the Snows of Granville, 25 miles away to the east on the Annapolis River, were Scots and not related to the German Jim Snow who arrived in Digby County with Aaron Hardy.

"The Granville Snows show the Scotch that is right in them," Bob said. "They are a different shape people altogether."

Bob did not know the German family names that had become

"Hardy" and "Snow" by the time they reached Smiths Cove. His own name and family origin also were German, the family name "Kosuth" somehow turned into "Cossett." His family had come to Nova Scotia "about the time of the Hessians," and by way of Montreal, a generation or two before the Hardys and Jim Snow.

The local oral history offered to me by Bob Cossett is the form of human history that probably has been most important to small communities ever since people first walked the earth: earnest, imperfect, biased, opinionated, but also broadly correct and defining of who we were and are.

All the people and families who Bob remembered and recounted once had animated and sustained themselves on the small piece of land extending from the western edge of Smiths Cove to the Salt Pond on the Joggin, perhaps 200-300 acres in total. They arrived, flourished, perished, departed or went crazy by turns, married each other and survived over a stretch of 150 years. The land is mostly forest again now, no longer pushed and pulled to grow food and fibre to nourish and house its settlers, but left to restore itself.

Carl Miller

In 1930, and again in 1931, I spent several summer months alone in the woods, learning about research in natural science by doing two small studies, first at remote Dish Lake, where I tried to identify the components of its ecosystem, and then at Loud Lake, a short carry and paddle up a deadwater from the Tom Wallace Road in Morganville, studying the behaviour of beavers. To do this work, I required official permission and good advice, and I received both from Carl Miller.

Carl was the Forest Ranger and Game Warden for a large area centred on Bear River. He was in his sixties at this time, strong, tall and handsome, the father of five sons. His wife, whom I knew only as Mrs. Miller, also was tall and good-looking, with a graceful and gentle manner. Before marrying Carl, she had run two millinery shops, one in Bear River and another in Annapolis Royal.

The Millers' home was a tall white house shaded by still-taller sugar maples on high ground at the north end of Bear River village.

Carl 's father and grandfather had been land owners and lumber operators at a time when lumbering was doing very well. Carl still owned a considerable part of his family's once-extensive properties. From time to time, he would take me into the woods to see this or that natural wonder—a quiet stand of hemlock, for instance, or a beaver dam five feet high—and he would comment casually that he owned the place where we were standing.

One of his sons, who did not much care for the woods, once

complained to me that "We've always been land-poor", by which he meant that the family did not have much to live on after paying all their property taxes.

People referred to Carl occasionally as "Major Miller" because he had held that rank in the army, and he carried himself with an upright military bearing. At the same time, there was an air of caution about him and an unwillingness to take chances, characteristics I have noted in other men of action who have survived.

He was expert with an axe, but very aware of its edges. One of the things he taught me was that when you use this tool, no matter how much of a hurry you are in, nor how small the job, you should always take the time to clear away bushes and branches for at least six feet on all sides and behind. An axe deflected in mid-swing can cut off a foot.

Carl's most outstanding skill as a woodsman, however, was in handling a canoe. He did not go in for racing, but he was the only person I ever knew who could paddle the 15 twisted, rock-strewn miles from Lake Joli to Little Dish Lake and never let his canoe canvas be scored by a rock. He could pass among those myriad hidden edges of sharp granite like a bat among trees in the night. If he did bump a rock even ever so slightly, he would wince as if the canoe's skin was his own.

Carl's language was as clean as his appearance. For expletives, "gracious" was about as far as he would go. He had a large stock of phrases to express enthusiasm, of which his favourite cry was, "My body and soul!"

He was not by any means unique among local men in his refusal to swear. There seemed to be two general classes of speakers in those days, those who, like Carl, adhered to "gracious" or, on very bad occasions, "bless gracious"; and those who employed without restraint a rich vocabulary of swearing and blasphemy.

Carl Miller did not smoke or drink. No doubt he had done his share of hunting, fishing and trapping, but he was unusual among the region's men of the woods in that he talked little about his adventures and prowess in animal slaughter. He liked to watch the doings of animals far more than knocking them over for some reason. For me, he was a good companion with whom to share trips in the woods, which we did for many years.

One day, he held our canoe silent and motionless for half an hour while we watched a cow moose and calf at the mouth of White Sand Stream.

Carl's greatest enthusiasm was for trees. They came into his stories about "timber cruising" in the old days when lumber camps had wooden chimneys made of logs and mud, and bread was baked in reflector ovens in front of their hearth. His eye was sharp for birch or pine of splendid age and proportions, and the sight of one would induce inarticulate cries and "my-body-and-souls" as he slapped the trunk and gazed up at the crown and told how many board feet were standing there as a way of expressing the wonder of it. Carl responded to trees the way others might respond to cathedrals.

A cathedral tree.

Bill Harris

For my summer study of beavers at Loud Lake, I needed an assistant who could care for the camp, cut fire wood, cook the meals, build cages and help in other ways. I asked Carl Miller, and he proposed Bill Harris. It was a wonderful recommendation, as it turned out. Bill was well-suited to the work and our relationship quickly moved from formal and awkward to friendship.

Bill was about thirty-five years old, short, heavy-set and sharp-featured. He lived with his wife and two sons, aged eight and ten, in a small house on the crest of the Lansdowne ridge above Bear River, looking out over the great expanse of wooded hills. He'd had very little formal education but was smart and a problem-solver, and was thoughtfully observant.

Bill earned wages working on farms and in lumber camps, and cutting forestry survey lines. He supplemented this income with deer hunting, a trap line and trout fishing.

At one point, Bill had tried working in "the Boston States" as an ice delivery man, which involved driving a horse and wagon about the streets, delivering ice from door to door. It required lugging heavy chunks of ice up numerous stair steps to kitchens and then lifting them up as high as his shoulders to get them into the top compartments of ice boxes. Bill told me he had enjoyed this work because he found the customers and their children friendly. One lady always had a beer waiting for him on hot summer days, and numerous children followed the wagon to get chips of ice on which to suck.

Bill did not remain very long in Boston, however, even though he "made good money". The city was not for him. "I missed them old trees," he said, "so I come home."

We had many talks alongside the campfire at Loud Lake. Gradually he told me more and more about his family, his friends and his neighbours, about his feelings and about life in and around Bear River. His boys often came along with him for a day at Loud Lake and once or twice his wife came as well.

It was through my many conversations with Bill that I first came to perceive that he felt a dread of the woods, a deep feeling I later found to be shared by many other forest-edge settlers. This was not a rational, targeted fear, such as the risk of getting lost. Nor was it fear of bears, although it was sometimes expressed that way. It was more a dread of the woods in their totality, like fear of a haunted house rather than of any particular ghost you might find within it.

Bill loved the edge of the woods and was comfortable in any place he could walk to and from in the same day. His hunting, trapping and fishing all were in that range of distance. He had never gone into the woods any deeper than this, not even with surveyor teams and logging gangs, and he had no desire to do so. As he might have said himself, there was not enough tea in China to pay him to stay out there alone. He even had trouble staying overnight at Loud Lake by himself.

A second and related source of fear was the dark of night. Even at his home and small farm, going outdoors at night was something he avoided as much as possible. The thought of being in the woods alone and in the dark was terrifying.

Through Bill's thoughtful comments and observations, I came to see that the local society of which the Harrises were a part was isolated by more than geography and lack of economic resources.

It thought and felt about things in ways that largely barred any internal widening of its own horizons, and that limited relations between itself and the larger society of which it also was a part.

One example was their concept of the resources of the earth. As they saw it, these were, by God's will, unlimited, inexhaustible and put on earth precisely for their use. Thus, all conservation efforts and regulations were either just misguided foolishness or actual wickedness, a form of deliberate persecution directed against the poor and intended to keep them that way. They saw the land, the forest and its products as they saw sunlight. You cannot use them up. That is how God made the world.

> There's always goin' to be enough game, and God gave us a right to them when we need them. It's in the Bible. That's how we get our meat in winter, and a little cash from the furs when there ain't no work or farmin' to do. And about them logs, if a man owns a woodlot, he's got the right to cut it the way he wants to, when he wants to.

These were their beliefs, but also their illusions. Even in the 1920s, this was not so. The caribou on the barrens of Digby County already had vanished within living memory, and so had the pine marten and the fisher. The great white pine forests all had been cut so that lumbering was now, as everyone said, a dwindling source of livelihood. "Just small stuff."

Closely tied to these beliefs about the fruits of the earth was a set of moral positions on game wardens, forestry officials, and the police. To Bill and his community, these were feeble specimens of humanity, hired by "them" to push the poor around and deprive them of their rights. Individual game wardens and policemen might not be such bad fellows. Indeed, "Some of them is pretty good," Bill once remarked.

They don't give you no trouble unless they have to, because someone has made a complaint, and then they mostly try to let you know in advance before they come. It's just too bad them fellers couldn't get no better kind of job. Sometimes there is something wrong, you know, gassed in the war or something, and they ain't fit for a real job.

But when a feller takes on work like that, I always think he's a traitor. That's why I can't understand about Carl Miller, why he done it. I always thought he was a good feller.

One of Carl 's sons told me that at school he had been in many fights because of his father's job. It seemed that, in the eyes of the settlers close to the woods, to be an officer of the law was to hold a contemptible position. Virtue in that post consisted in taking the pay and not doing the work. The only conceivable value in a game warden was to use him to get back at a neighbour, if you were that mean.

A hero to Bill was his uncle, Truman Hamilton, who had been a famous lumber camp cook, with skills in human relations and management as well as in kneading dough and frying hash. A favoured sport among lumbermen was to torment the cook, and on one occasion Uncle Trume's clients got out of hand, throwing bread on the floor for the fun of watching him sweep it up. It started as if by accident, but soon the floor was littered. This was the same bread that Uncle Trume got up at four o'clock every morning to bake.

He endured the behaviour for several meals, sweeping busily away in silence. Then, the next day, he appeared to appeal to the men's better nature by offering a sumptuous and favourite dessert, bread pudding with lots of raisins and molasses.

When the men had finished, and had got to the tooth-picking

stage, he beat a skillet with a ladle for silence. His announcement, cleaned up a bit, went something like this:

> Now, you dogs, I just want to tell you that you just et all the stuff you throwed on the floor yesterday, mixed up with the mud and the horse shit off your boots. If any of you want to make somethin' of it, I'll be outside the front door and take you on one at a time when you come out.

Whereupon he snatched off his apron, dashed to the front of the shanty and stood there bare-armed, his fists at the ready.

There was nothing but silence inside for a time and then the men began to emerge and slink away. Some went into the bushes to puke, but none of them took up Uncle Trume's challenge. Meal times thereafter were orderly.

In addition to opinions, attitudes and ideas about many fundamental things that were very different from mine, the Harrises, together with their network of friends and neighbors, had a different style of speaking. By the standards of my family and friends, the number of words at their command was small and their grammar terrible, *i.e.*, much simpler in its rules but also less able to make distinctions.

"I know I don't speak proper," Bill said to me one day. "I know I shouldn't say ain't and 'them logs' and 'them beavers'; it ought to be 'those logs' and 'those beavers'; and I ought to say 'going' instead of 'goin', but if I was to speak like you, I'd have to move away from home. I wouldn't have no friends no more, couldn't fit in. They'd think I was big feelin'."

It struck me that this applied not just to speaking style, but to the totality of Bill's ideas, opinions and beliefs. Holding these was necessary to have a peaceful and inclusive life in his community, but it also helped lock the community into many of the conditions they most bitterly resented, including poverty.

'Thing' was a favourite word in Bill's community. It was applied to animate objects. A horse or cow or ox was often referred to as 'the thing', as in "the thing would not hold still" or "the thing bit me." This became a humorous dig when applied to a person. For example, a wife might say to one of the children, "Go tell your father to come in or the thing won't get his dinner."

I was therefore not a little intrigued to discover, by accidental eavesdropping, that in the Harris family, I was known as "the thing".

A refuge from the night.

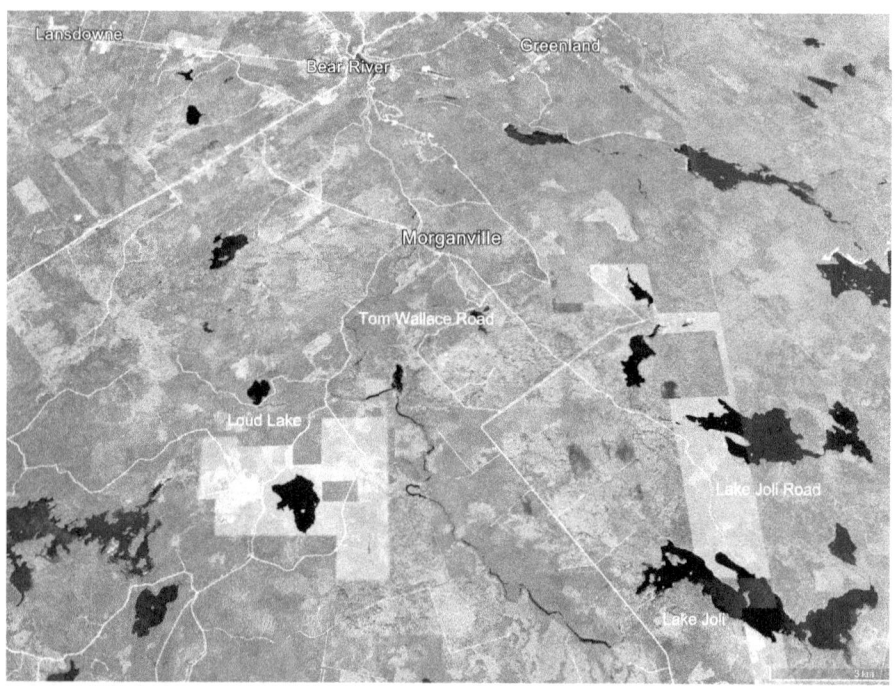

Bear River-Morganville

Boudica

In 1931, I studied the behaviour of beavers as a research project required of my undergraduate program of studies in biology at Princeton University. In this work, I was guided by Professor Edwin Grant Conklin, from whom I learned much about what science is and is not.

I practised and honed skills in collecting objective information and in distinguishing it, as much as possible, from pre-formed notions and assumptions. These research skills served me well. Ultimately, I was granted my degree, and I published my small study of beavers in a scientific journal. However, I learned much more from the beavers that summer than just some useful research skills.

I conducted my study at Loud Lake, near Morganville, south of Bear River. This lake got its name from the great echo produced when any shout or noise was made there.

Bill Harris worked with me that long and busy summer, ferrying in food and materials, building cages, tending the camp and carefully recording beaver observations. You can drive to Loud Lake now, on a branch off the Tom Wallace Road, but in 1931, you could not. From the Tom Wallace Road, we had to carry everything needed about 400 yards on a forest trail to reach a deadwater, along which we then could paddle a canoe another half mile to reach the lake.

I had expected all beavers to be about the same, each one an example of "the beaver," varying in behaviour somewhat according to age and sex, perhaps, but not by much else. As part of the work, we live-trapped three beavers and held them in side-by-side cages. The hope was that we would be able to observe some of their behaviour in detail and at close range, even though the context of captivity was highly unnatural.

We did, indeed, learn many lessons from these captive beavers, "my beavers" as I shamelessly came to think of them. In particular, I learned that the commonly-held notion that intellectual superiority and the capacity to exercise free will separates humans from all other creatures is nonsense. The evidence was otherwise.

The first beaver we trapped we named Tony. Based on size, we thought he was a yearling, just entering his second summer, a large animal but not fully adult size.

Tony seemed to have read up on beaver behaviour as understood by biologists in 1931 and he behaved precisely as expected. He spent three quarters of his time in the water at the southeast corner of his pen, where it extended into the lake. He seemed the very image of stolidity cast in beaver. The rest of the time, he plodded through all the feeding, brushing, diving and tail-slapping behaviours described in the literature.

Tony was willing to eat out of my hand, but his manner was neither friendly nor hostile, just pragmatic. It took me some time to recognize that he was left-handed. The beavers I observed elsewhere on Loud Lake seemed always to manipulate food and other objects as if they were right-handed. Tony was different.

The second beaver we were able to capture and observe turned out to be one of the current year's brood, a "kitten" not more than a few months old. We called him "Beejy", which was our approximation of a Mi'kmaw word I was told meant "little beaver".

Beejy was much livelier, more responsive and cuter than Tony, and was always busy about something. Whatever he was doing, whether brushing his fur or nibbling bark, his bright little eyes made contact with yours, very much like a child or a puppy. Although he was frisky, I could not induce him to play with me, and I never saw him try to play with Tony.

Thus, Tony and Beejy were quite different as individual beavers, but it seemed likely that, except for left versus right handedness, the differences were related to age.

The next beaver we captured taught us much about the personality differences among beavers. She was taken in a corral trap during a night when I was away from camp and Bill Harris was on duty by himself. He wrote about it as follows in our daily log book.

> 3:00 AM
>
> She was putting up a big fight to get out and had been digging at the lake end of the trap on the left side of the door. She had a hole she could drive her head under, but her body was too big. She was very cross and showed fight as soon as I stepped up to the trap.
>
> I took some boards and drove them into the mud with an axe inside of the wire where she had been digging. She took the boards in her teeth and paws, pulled them up and threw them to one side. Then I drove them in on the outside and ran for a box.
>
> When I got back, she was digging in a new place. I lowered the box into the trap, but she would not have it in there. She stood up on her hind legs and with her front feet and head stopped the box from going on the ground, and she started pitching it about in the pen. I could not do a thing with the box.
>
> I stood on guard until daylight, and then I went to the tents and got a rope. I tried to lasso her, but she caught it with her hands every time. I threw a short stick at her, and

she caught it in her hands too and sat up and began chewing it. I managed then to get the lasso over her shoulders, and I tossed another half hitch and got her again in the same place.

I pulled her up to the trap wire and got her by the hind feet and the back of the neck. I carried her to the pen and turned her loose in it. She made a bolt for the water and struck the wire at the water end with such force that she turned over backwards. She did this a couple more times and then began swimming about.

This was a different beaver! I named her "Boudica" after a queen of the ancient Britons who is reputed to have personally led her woad-blue troops into battle against the Romans. She is also said to have attached scythe blades to the wheels of her war chariots to slice the legs of the Roman infantry.

At its on-land end, the pen in which Boudica was placed had an artificial house made of sods. She disappeared into this soon after capture and for the next few weeks remained there during most daylight hours. Under cover of dark, she would emerge and, after eating the food provided, she would spend most of her time trying to rip down her pen.

Touching Boudica with bare hands, our usual practice with the other captive beavers, was out of the question. In addition to raw violence, she employed trickery. There were nights when she would sit out in the water, much like Tony, creating the impression that she had given up on fighting and lapsed, like him, into wooden indifference. This lasted only long enough to let us be a little unguarded, at which point she would rush out of the water and head for our legs with her scythe blades flashing.

Like the other beavers, Boudica mostly was a slow mover on land, but she was capable of instant take-off into high speed for a

dash of about four feet. There were times when she would pro-
gress along a line diagonal to where one of us was standing, looking as if she was intent on going somewhere else. When she got to
a point in this trajectory that was about four feet away, she would
suddenly wheel and charge.

Bill and I never got bitten, partly due to good luck and partly because Boudica's aim when fast-moving was not very precise, and she
slashed pant legs instead of flesh and bone. Twice, due to my jumping
away, she bit herself, once gashing her tail so that it bled considerably.

Among the three captive beavers, Boudica alone was able to sum-
mon the others. Normally, each of the beavers seemed just to do their
own thing in their cages and never seemed to congregate or interact
with each other in any way.

I saw and heard this summons one night while Boudica was at the
lake-end of her pen and Tony and Beejy were some distance away on
land in each of theirs. Boudica uttered a sound that was different from
any I had previously heard from a beaver, and instantly the other two
hurried into the water and swam to positions as close to her as the
placement of the cages would accommodate.

The life-long lesson I learned from Tony, Beejy and Boudica was
to beware of all thinking in stereotypes. They all were beavers, to
be sure, and could be recognized as such by all the attributes we
imply by the word "beaver." But they also were unique individuals
with their own divergent traits and personalities that even I, with
my very limited knowledge of beavers, could recognize.

Human prejudice is based on thinking in stereotypes, in assum-
ing that each individual of the "other" that we choose to disdain is
more or less identical. This is not true, even among beavers, and
puts the lie to all the justifications of prejudice ever invented.

Boudica admiring the bronze statue of Boudica, the Celtic queen, and her daughters, on a war chariot, by the English sculptor Thomas Thorneycroft, completed in 1885 and erected at the western end of Westminster Bridge, London, England in 1902.

Michael Finnegan

When I began spending time in and around Bear River, starting about 1920, I heard many stories about Michael Finnegan, or "Buster" Finnegan as he was known to most people. He was the bad man about town, with a reputation for violence carried out on a background of senseless jokes and malarkey.

Michael lived alone on an abandoned farm at the edge of Morganville. The house had weathered away on the outside and was collapsing on the inside, and the forest was advancing into the fields that once had been the sustenance of a settler family. From this home base, Michael sold illegal booze, generated famous drunken parties, and in various other ways built up a reputation for his place as a haven for hellions.

The first time I heard of Michael Finnegan was when I learned that my friend Harlan Louis was found dead down Michael's well, and Michael was suspected of his murder. Harlan was a good-natured, easy-going, roly-poly man from the Mi'kmaq community, with an impressive walrus moustache. He built canoes in his living room and guided sport fishermen and hunters.

The news of Harlan's death was an ugly shock to many people, including me, and different accounts to explain what had happened, and who was to blame, quickly sprang up in the community. The one given widest credibility at the time was that, at a drinking party at Michael's house, Michael had become enraged at Harlan for drinking more than he could pay for. He had beaten

Harlan unconscious with a club and then stuffed him head-first down the well. There were no witnesses willing to talk.

An alternate explanation, and the final official view, was that Harlan had gone to the well for a drink of water and had fallen in.

A story about Michael Finnegan that became a legend in Bear River began with Michael returning from a trip somewhere and falling off the train and onto the Bear River Station platform in a drunken stupor.

The station was some four miles from the village. As soon as the taxi driver, who customarily met the trains, perceived Michael's condition, he loaded the other passengers into his vehicle and took off, leaving those at the station to figure out what to do with the drunk.

The only means of transportation remaining was a flat-bed truck used for freight, and it appeared certain that, if Michael were placed on that, he would roll off during the journey and be maimed or killed. There were those who thought that such an opportunity should not have been missed, but an empty crate was spotted on the station platform. It was quickly re-built, with Michael inside it, and hoisted onto the truck. In this cage, he was driven, up, down, through and around Bear River.

Micheal appeared to enjoy the notoriety, reaching out through the bars with a bottle, offering drinks, yelling, singing, and making obscene gestures.

As a result of Harlan's death and stories like this, I formed an impression of Michael Finnegan as a massive man of great violence. According to local gossip, he had beaten up many people, including his father and his brother.

The father, Trumpington Finnegan, lived in a hut under a huge, crooked white pine at a bend in the Tom Wallace Road, not far from where the trail began for the Loud Lake Deadwater. He seemed very lonely and aged, and glad of some company when I would drop in for a visit during my summer with the beavers on Loud Lake. On the subject of Michael, however, he was silent.

Carl Miller told me Trumpington was deathly afraid of his son, who had it in for him for mistreating his mother. Other people said that none of the rest of the family except his brother, Tom, would have anything to do with Michael.

I met Michael Finnegan in person at Loud Lake in the summer of 1931, when, unexpectedly, he walked into my camp for the first of what would be several visits. I was astonished at how different he appeared from what I had imagined. He was short, thin, and frail-looking. During one visit, he told me he was the runt of the family litter.

If all the assault stories were true, he must have been capable of turning himself into a screaming fury, swarming up on top of people like a weasel, pounding their heads, gouging their eyes, and kicking every soft part he could reach.

As I saw him around Loud Lake, he always carried a gun. It was only a .22, but still, deadly enough. I imagine he kept it handy for any small game he might chance to see. I wondered if he also carried it as a stage prop to enhance the label of violence which his community, and perhaps he himself, had attached to him.

Bill Harris told me that the only person in the world Michael Finnegan cared about was his mother. Even this was impulsive rather than steady. He would give her money when he happened to have some, or show up one day and do all the wash for her, or scrub the kitchen floor.

He was also said to be generous to some of the children in the family, giving them cash presents. I once saw him hold out an American quarter to a little boy, while telling him, "Watch out the eagle don't shit in yer pocket."

On his visits to my camp on Loud Lake, Michael's manner was quiet and the expression on his thin, sharp-chinned face was solemn, his mouth with down-drawn corners even when he was making his frequent vulgar jokes. At those times, he had a powerful aura of melancholy, but not of violence.

There is a legend in the folklore of the Ukraine about a young man, Ivan Mazepa, whose crime of passion is punished severely by the cuckold Count. He is stripped naked and lashed to the back of a horse, which then is tormented into madness and released to run wild. Mazepa goes through what seems like a lifetime of misery, torture and near-death experiences, and can exert no control over his circumstances.

As I think back to my encounters with Michael Finnegan, I wonder if his life, like that of young Ivan Mazepa, was compelled forward by something he had been fastened to that was not of his own choosing. I can imagine that Michael's wild horse might have been some mix of childhood traumas, mental illness, poverty and social ostracism except when he would perform as an unsavoury clown.

The Crossing

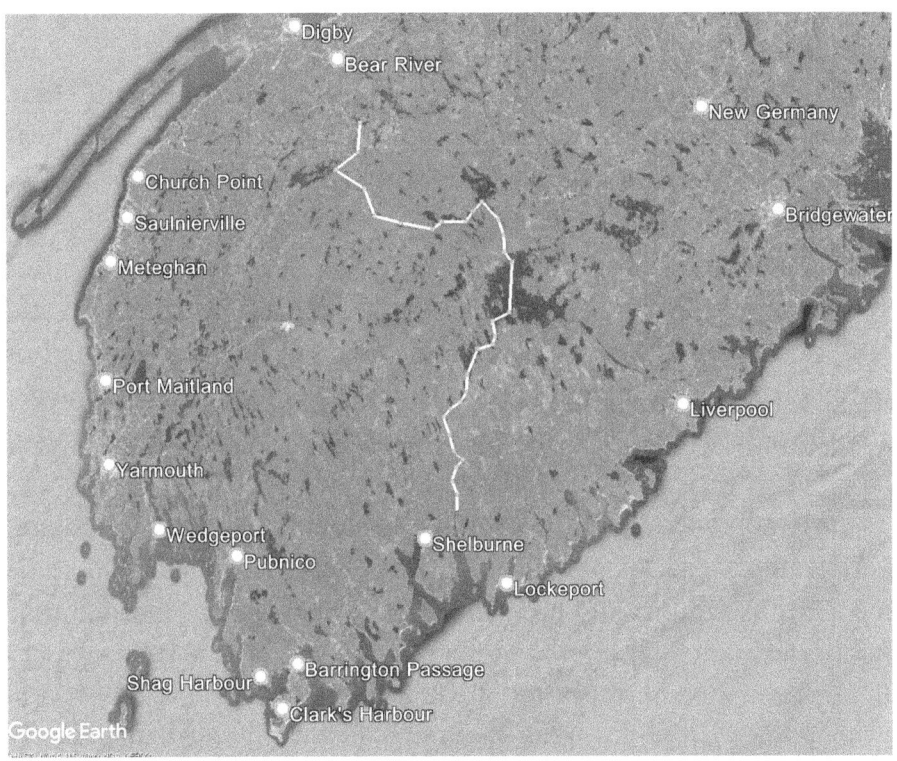

In the spring of 1927, I asked Billy Meuse if he would guide me on a trip by canoe and carry from Lake Joli, close to Bear River, all the way south across Nova Scotia to its southern shore, a straight-line distance of 50 miles and about 80 miles of actual travel along the twisting pathways of the forest.

Billy Meuse was one of my boyhood heroes, along with several other Mi'kmaq men who had guided me on camping trips into the Bear River and Sissiboo River watersheds over the previous eight years, among them Louie Peters, Harlan Louis, Peter Glode, and John McEwan, who brought along his son Richard as a companion of my own age. I was in awe of their skills with canoes and woodcraft and wilderness navigation, and with their total joy and comfort living within and from the forest. I came to know and to respect and to love these men, and to cherish the mentorship they offered me.

Billy Meuse took a week to decide whether or not he would take on this long-distance guiding job, and then said he would. The water in the lakes and rivers was high that summer, ideal for such travel. We would depart in mid-June.

I was not quite 19 years old in June 1927. It was a moment of great anxiety in my personal life. My schooling had been erratic and mostly done through private tutors. Now I was at the end of the high school curriculum and wanted very much to go to university to study biology. I especially wanted to go to Princeton University in New Jersey.

Princeton had high admission requirements that included doing very well on a series of college entrance examinations. I had studied for those exams and had taken them, but in May I learned that my performance on them had been lower than I knew was expected by Princeton of its potential students.

I had no Plan B to follow after I received what I was sure would be a letter of rejection from Princeton. I felt sullen and morose and without direction. A long stretch of canoe camping in the Nova Scotia forest suggested itself as a distraction that might help me recover from my big disappointment and move on.

On hearing of this, my same-age cousin from Belfast, Will Leighton, declared himself game to join me for some Canadian wilderness adventure, and he came to Nova Scotia in early June. We decided we would prepare ourselves for the journey by spending a few weeks camping in the familiar Sissiboo watershed before setting out to traverse the province with Billy Meuse.

Will and I established a base for wilderness explorations at what then was known as the Osburn camp on Whitesand Stream. It had been built as a satellite camp for sports—tourist hunters and fishermen—who were hosted initially at a much larger and more elegant lodge on Sixth Lake, seven canoe-and-carry miles closer to civilization. This lodge itself was an inland satellite of the tourist hotel and cabins at Smiths Cove, on the Annapolis Basin, known as Harbour View.

In 1927, the Osburn camp consisted of two cabins for sports, one for guides and a cooking shed. From this base camp, Will and I were taken here and there on day trips, and sometimes overnight, by our guide, Louie Peters.

Visitors periodically came to the Osburn camp, including my mother and sister for a short stay. Our most memorable foray from the base camp was a two-day visit to Dish and Flagstaff lakes. I often had heard of Dish Lake, but I never had been there. To me, it seemed the very essence of deep wilderness.

It was easy to reach from the Osburn camp, up Whitesand Stream a short way to a mile-long carry to the Dish Lake deadwater, and then a paddle up the deadwater to the lake. After exploring the lake, we landed on its south shore and Louie Peters took us on a hike southward over a small height of land to tiny Flagstaff Lake, the water from which trickled down to join the Shelburne River and onward south to the Atlantic Ocean. Soon we also would follow the Shelburne.

Near the north end of Flagstaff Lake was an enormous rock, flat-topped and as big as a house. The land surrounding much of Dish and Flagstaff lakes in 1927 was "barrens," large, open plains of low bushes, mosses and lichens, with a few small trees that grew only in low, wet hollows. Caribou had helped maintain this landform for millennia, it must be supposed, but they became extinct a few decades earlier. Trees were just beginning to close in and bushes to overgrow the lichen fields.

Flagstaff Rock stood high, a massive presence above the barrens, and we all scrambled up its steep sides for the magnificent view. We had not come prepared to camp at Flagstaff Lake, but we spent so much time there that Louie Peters built us a lean-to shelter of poles and brush and we spent the night in it together before walking back to Dish Lake in the morning, and then on to the Osburn camp.

Forever after this first visit, I was enthralled with Dish Lake, with its forests, and bogs and fens and deadwater and barrens. In my heart, it became my personal axis, my fixed point on earth around which the rest of my life and work would rotate and be held in place.

Three years later, I would return to spend a summer there, learning about nature, science and loneliness. In six years more, I would return with my new bride on our honeymoon. Twenty years further on, I would return with my children, and on my 90th birthday, when I no longer was able to travel in the forest myself, I would have myself flown in to spend one more night there, to offer that place a final greeting and farewell.

Somehow, across all that time, it has retained its essence of wilderness.

We were to depart on our cross-Nova Scotia trek on a Monday morning. Billy Meuse and his chosen porter and helper had come out to the Osburn camp with all of our supplies, and we were to leave the next day. I arose early that morning, still feeling the sting of those poor test grades and their troublesome implications for my future. I went for a swim in the stream in front of the camp and climbed out on a streamside rock to dry off in the morning sun.

I was roused from my despondency by the sight of a canoe and two paddlers who came into view downstream around a bend and worked their way up to me in hurried strokes. They asked me who I was and, on hearing my name, looked relieved and held out to me an envelope.

This I opened and found within a telegram sent to me from Princeton University, telling me I had been *accepted* as a student for the fall of 1927. My mother had received the telegram in Smiths Cove, and had immediately engaged two strong paddlers to get me the message before I disappeared to no known location in the forest.

I relived that glorious moment of relief, joy and happiness a thousand times over the next eighty years. The clouds that had darkened my spirits for so many weeks suddenly were swept away.

We were a travelling party of five in two canoes. Billy Meuse had chosen Dube Rice as his sous chef. Dube may have had a different name also, but I only ever heard him called Dube. He lived in the last inhabited house on the Lake Joli Road and was a ship caulker by trade. Caulking wooden ships to prevent leaks was called "dubing" locally, so perhaps this explains his name.

Billy and Dube each steered and managed one of the two canoes from the stern, and Will and I provided horsepower by paddling from our seats in the bow. The fifth participant was my fully-grown Newfoundland dog, Fubsy.

Our canoes had been built in Bear River by John McEwan, of wood and canvas. They were large and, by today's standards, very heavy. We carried a lot of cargo. Camping food in 1927 mostly came in cans—meat, fish, beans, also food for a 150-pound dog. We had lighter foods, too, such as porridge oats, hard-tack bread, tea, and sugar. The canoes were heavily laden, especially at the start, and several trips had to be made across each carry.

Our food and gear were packed mostly in baskets woven of thin strips of ash wood. These we carried on our backs with tumplines across our foreheads to bear some of the weight. We carried no tent, but slept under the canoes in blankets. We cooked on small, quickly-made wood fires.

There were few blackflies, and the mosquitoes were at their normal background level of tolerable annoyance. There was no effective insect repellent in those days, but we sometimes applied citronella oil for this purpose, which works for a few minutes until the oil evaporates. Dog ticks and deer ticks had not yet found their way to Nova Scotia in 1927, so we encountered none.

I brought with me a 16mm movie camera, tripod and cans of film. Movie cameras for personal use had come on the market in the early 1920s, and I had become an ardent home movie-maker. The camera was large and heavy, and had to be cranked by hand, but with it I was able to document much of the journey.

I lugged along this heavy, awkward, but marvellous movie camera for my own fun and enjoyment, but over time the films I took have had some wider value also, documenting the remarkable skills of real people in real places, now almost 100 years ago. Digitized copies now are in many homes on the Bear River First Nation and also in the Provincial archives.

Billy Meuse learned to apply his own steady hand to the movie camera, so I myself appear in a few scenes.

The route we took across Nova Scotia easily can be traced and followed today. We put the canoes in the water at Lake Joli, Digby County and took them out at the end of the journey on the shore of the Jordan River near the town of Jordan Falls, Shelburne County. From Lake Joli, we carried into tiny Ninth Lake on the Sissiboo River watershed and then through Eighth, Seventh and Sixth lakes to Sixth Lake Stream and down to Fifth Lake, and up Whitesand Stream to the Osburn camp, where we dallied a while.

When Billy Meuse and Dube Rice joined us, we travelled upstream from the Osburn camp to Whitesand Lake, then to the

Moosehead River and on to Moosehead Lake (now these more often are called Moosehide River and Lake). From here, we carried
across the two-mile-long Coufan carry over the watershed divide
to the shore of the Shelburne River and then travelled eight twisty
miles down stream to a brook that led up into Pebbeloggitch Lake,
just inside what is now, but was not then, the southwest boundary
of Kejimkujik National Park. We crossed parts of Peskawa,
Peskowesk, and Mountain lakes to reach Kejimkujik Lake, and then
paddled south to its outlet as the Mersey River at Eel Weir.

From Eel Weir to Jordan Falls, we would be going down rapids
most of the way. We paused to check over the canoes and to cut
and assemble "snubbing poles", the essential tool for navigating
shallow rapids in a canoe. Billy Meuse patched small rents in the
canvas with a mixture of rosin (pitch) and shellac. Pitch alone
would crack and fall away.

The snubbing poles were made from carefully-selected standing
small, dead spruce trees. These were found in dense stands of
young spruce among which competition for light and soil was
fierce. The losers in this growth competition were dead but com-
posed of sound, solid wood; thin, light and dry.

Billy peeled and shaped them with axe and crooked knife. He
had brought with him the metal fittings that made a spruce pole
into a snubbing pole: a long heavy spike and a solid metal collar.
He split the wide end of the spruce pole enough to insert deeply
one end of the spike, then brought the collar down from the thin
end of the pole to fit tightly around the wider end with its protruding spike, forcing the sides of the split end together in a secure grip
around the spike.

To navigate rapids, Billy and Dube would stand in the canoe
each was in charge of, and use the snubbing pole against the
stream bottom to direct the canoe this way and that, while Will
and I in the bow of each canoe either paddled as directed or

cowered down out of the way of the pole.

Fubsy was the model canoe traveller. He was required to lie in his place in the canoe and not move around, and he did so, sometimes for hours, shifting position ever so gently when the need arose. He ran the carry trails with delight and swam at every opportunity.

We raced down the Mersey River to Lake Rossignol with little effort, and there Billy encountered a man in a motor boat, whom he engaged to tow us across the big open-water lake. We thus were ferried down to the SW corner of Rossignol, and we then proceeded diagonally across Coade, Sixth, Silver, Jordan, Rush and Randy lakes to Lake John and its outlet as the Jordan River, which we followed to the sea.

During that whole traverse of Nova Scotia, I marvelled at how perfectly Billy Meuse knew the way. He knew precisely where each carry began and ended and we then would paddle directly to the next one on a distant shore, never needing to cruise a shoreline looking for a trail. He anticipated every rapid we encountered, knew how it turned and tumbled and what obstacles it might contain to damage a canoe or drown its occupants.

This was the more surprising to me when he told me, at the end of the trip, that he himself never previously had travelled much of our route. When I had asked him if he would guide us on this crossing, he had gone to Mi'kmaq elders in Bear River and asked them if it could be done and what routes could be taken. Collectively, they did know the way, and told him he could go there. They were able explain the route to him in a vocabulary so specific and precise that Billy knew the way with complete confidence even though he himself had never before travelled south of Kejimkujik Lake.

I went to study at Princeton in the fall of 1927. Will returned to Belfast and eventually became an actor on stage and screen, based in London. I did not travel the Nova Scotia forests with Billy Meuse or Dube Rice again.

During the many trips into the woods I took with Mi'kmaq guides, I studied their skills and knowledge as deeply as I could, with full attention, but my learning always seemed shallow and incomplete. Generally, I felt as ignorant travelling the woods with them as I had felt ignorant when I did so poorly on those college entrance exams.

Toward the end of this crossing, though, I felt a change in Billy Meuse's attitude toward me. Perhaps it was only in my imagination, but as we lifted our canoes out of the Jordan River, Billy spoke to me as though I had come to the end of a long apprenticeship and thereby had achieved some low level of genuine entry into his guild of knowledge and woodcraft. He had accepted me then as a kind of novice, willing and able from now on to learn to guide myself, on my own.

Louie Penny

Louie Penny was the terror that lurked in the woods. He was a gangly, horrible giant of a man, equal parts bear and pirate. He lived alone in brush camps and caves and rock crevices. He preyed on travellers, stole from and plundered the settlers of the forest fringe, murdered whomever he pleased and amassed a vast treasure. He moved about only at night. He left a trail of fear and destruction wherever he went, but no living person ever had seen him.

He had haunted these woods as far back as anyone could remember. No one knew whether he lived here still, except my wife Dorothea and I, who had made up the whole story to create a little deception and adventure for our children, then aged 6-9.

It was the 1950s, and in those years, we spent a few weeks each summer using an old lumber-camp cook shack on Lake Joli as our woodland cabin. We would canoe around the lake and up and down its tributaries, walk down the West Branch to the bridge on the Indian Trail, and sometimes carry up Frankin Brook to the deadwater and camp for a day or two on one of Lake Franklin's sandy beaches.

There always was a dog or two with us. Once, as we were paddling up Ninth Lake Brook, a dog leapt out of the canoe onto the stream bank in pursuit of a muskrat, and the muskrat escaped by jumping into canoe.

You can pick up a muskrat by its long and hairless tail, and you are safe from being bitten for a while. However, within a few seconds, the muskrat will use its forepaws to grasp its belly fur and pull itself up, hand over hand, toward your hand so its sharp teeth might free it from the unwelcome grip.

Those few seconds were time enough to swing the dangling muskrat well clear of the canoe and let it drop into the brook. Getting the dog back into the canoe without mishap required more skill and ingenuity.

Our children became seasoned canoers and campers early on, without really noticing it, and felt as safe in the woods as they did in their usual home. To them, a fresh bear track was an excitement but no cause for alarm.

We could swim anywhere on Lake Joli, but our favourite spot was a small, sandy beach about 200 yards west of our cabin, on the edge of a small bay. We called it "Sandy Cove", and went to swim there on hot afternoons.

One of our dogs, we called him Fundy, was a rejected toller—a Nova Scotia Tolling Retriever. He didn't meet some physical requirements of the official breed, but his mind was 100% toller.

Tollers are supposed to play on a beach like a fox might do, to cause curious ducks to approach within shotgun range. Fundy did this day in and day out without need of ducks or hunters. If you brushed his nose with the tip of his own tail, he would chase that tail tip around and around in circles.

He was a mad digger also, digging up nothing in particular for long stretches of time, sometimes emitting quiet yips of delight deep into his holes.

One summer day at the "Sandy Cove" beach, Fundy's digging produced a surprise. From deep in his hole in the beach-side sand, he unearthed a small, narrow bottle, about five inches tall, which he cast aside as he continued to dig.

One of the children noticed the bottle and picked it up to see what it might be. We all gathered around.

The glass was a light amethyst lavender, but also was scratched and nearly opaque. The bottle was closed with a stopper held in place with sealing wax, and there was something inside it, an object that moved a little when the bottle was tilted or shaken.

The stopper quickly was removed. Inside the bottle was a piece of old-looking paper on which was scrawled a crude map of some kind. The map included a large "X" marked on one particular spot. Written on the map in a similarly crude hand was a simple declaration: "Louie Penny, His Treasure."

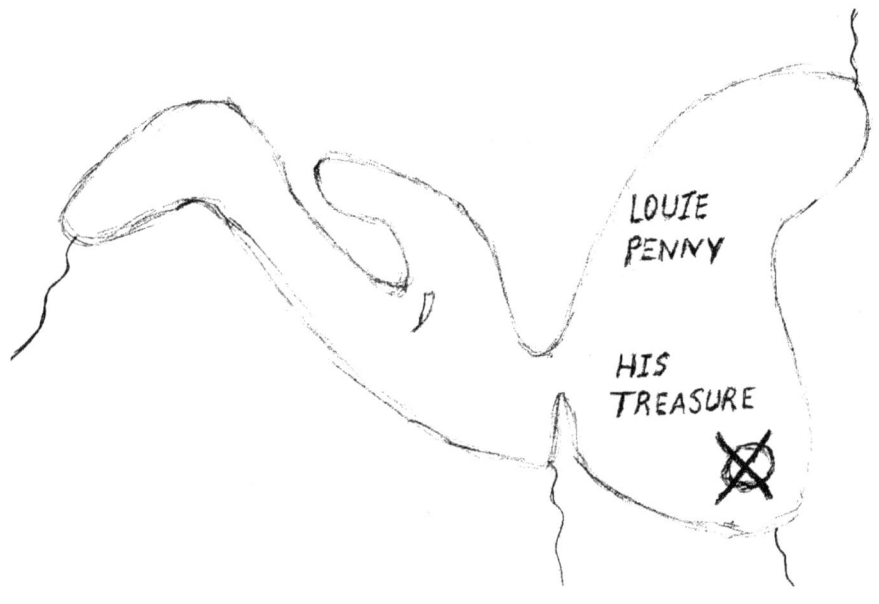

A map to a treasure! The children hardly could contain themselves. But who was Louie Penny?

As the map was taken from the bottle and unfolded, the personas of my wife and I became those of grave parental concern. We must not speak of this now, we said. We must smooth over the dog's hole to erase any evidence of digging at that location. We must speak no more to each other of our discovery. We must swim a while longer while the dog digs more and different holes, and then we must pack up our things and make our way back to the cabin, slowly and normally.

Only there, after dark, with blinds drawn and by lamplight, could we speak further of this matter.

The children got the message and could hardly breathe through their intense and anxious excitement.

Finally the moment came when the map could be placed on the table and considered again. As we studied it, I recited to the children all of Louie Penny's stark evil that my wife and I had invented. They were thrilled with the terror of it all.

The older children already were familiar with topographic maps, and they quickly discerned that the treasure map seemed to be of our own Lake Joli. The X was marked on a small island we had never visited, near what they knew to be the mouth of Franklin Brook.

"What should we do?" we asked the children.

The options ranged from setting out for Louie Penny's island immediately, armed with flashlights, to extinguishing the lamp and hiding in the dark shack until daylight when we might safely cross the lake and drive home.

Was Louie Penny still alive? Was he looking for us now? If we looked for the treasure, would we find him also?

The older children were able to convince themselves that Penny probably no longer was alive. If he had gone away, surely he would have taken his treasure with him. So it seemed safe, sort of, to go looking for it in the morning.

Thus, the terror and awful mystery gradually gave way to strategic and operational planning. The expedition must leave by canoe at a normal time for morning events, after breakfast and not too early. We would take two canoes, each with paddlers capable of rapid escape if the other was captured. We must bring digging tools carefully hidden in the bottom of the canoes. We must paddle around the island at least twice, observing everything observable, before venturing in to land and to explore.

The next morning, we followed the children's plan, expressing grave parental concern all the while.

The island remained impenetrable to our intense inspection as we circumnavigated it twice, revealing nothing to dampen or heighten our anxieties. At last we ventured in to shore.

The island was covered in tall spruce and granite boulders, and was surrounded entirely by a dense thicket of huckleberry bushes, hard to push a way through even for adults. There seemed only one place where canoes could approach the shore and land, and there was only one small area, perhaps three feet across, in which there was enough boulder-free ground to bury anything at all.

This seemed our only hope, so the children began to dig into it with trowels, looking furtively behind them and around them as they did so, as if Louie Penny might suddenly appear and pounce.

It was hard work and for a long time it offered no reward or encouragement. Eventually, however, off to one side of the chosen patch of ground, a trowel scraped against some hard object in loose soil about six inches below the surface.

All attention was riveted to the spot and small hands dug and scrabbled away the gravelly soil until the mouth of an earthenware jar was revealed, sealed completely with wax. It was wide and tall, and required much additional digging to dislodge, and it was a very heavy jar that required several hands to wiggle free and slowly raise up out of its burial pit.

When thus revealed, it was about a foot high and eight inches wide at its widest. Its sides had been glazed a medium brown, and written on one side were the words:

Louie Penny, His Jar

The wax seal on the mouth of the jar was quickly removed and the jar was found to be full of money. Real treasure!

The children could not believe their discovery. Right on top were six silver dollar coins, lying on a thin layer of smaller silver change. Beneath this layer, the jar was filled with pennies.

An ethical dilemma had come out of the ground with the jar. The children asked, "Are we now thieves ourselves, stealing Louie Penny's buried treasure?"

Was Louie Penny still alive? Was it "finders keepers" when it came to buried treasure? What was the right thing to do, take the treasure with us or put it back where we had found it?

I offered the view that Louie Penny must certainly have died many years ago, since the stories about him were very old and no one had heard or seen any signs of him for many decades.

Dorothea proposed that Louie Penny perhaps had no friends or family to whom he could leave his treasure, and that the map he had buried in a medicine bottle at "Sandy Cove" could be thought of as his will that might be discovered, or not, by some future forest-dweller and through which he might be remembered, or not, in the local communities he had lived beside.

So we took the jar with us, first back to our woodland cabin and then back to our home.

The children were more inclined to keep the silver dollars than to spend them. The rest of the money, like their fear of Louie Penny, quickly was forgotten, except by we who had to re-roll all those pennies.

Louie Penny was never forgotten, however. Sixty years later, his jar still has pride of place in our kitchen, and two more generations of children have heard the story, touched the jar, and know where to find Louie Penny's Island.

Like Evangeline, Louie Penny never existed. However, Evangeline has come to symbolize for the Acadians and many others the terrible expulsion of 1755 and all their associated suffering. In a smaller but similar way, for our family, Louie Penny gradually became a good and friendly spirit who was not evil, after all, but generous, and who must have loved the woods as we do.

We are less willing now to believe stories told about "evil" people who lurk at the edges of communities and societies. We are more inclined to think that such people are simply misunderstood by those who fear them, their "evil" a fantasy invented by others.

Curt Rice

The old cook shack that was my family's woodland cabin in the 1950s and 1960s was left over from the last of the tree cutting done by men and horses on the south side of Lake Joli, in the 1940s and 1950s. To get there, you could walk in five miles on the Indian Trail from its trailhead near the fire tower on Lake Joli Road, or you could cross the lake, starting at the public landing at the old Lake Joli town site, only half a mile by water.

I went there once in late November, with friend and helper John McGuire of Smiths Cove, to make some much-needed repairs. We drove out to the lake and rowed our boat across on a Saturday morning, intending to stay for several days. I had to be in Digby the following Monday afternoon for an appointment, but I planned go there directly from Lake Joli and return that same evening.

It snowed that weekend, a cold and early snowfall.

On Monday morning, John rowed me across the lake and left me at the landing while he went back to continue the carpentry work. I walked up the hill to where we had left the car, a middle-aged Volkswagen Beetle, but then discovered that it would not start.

My appointment was important, so I decided I would walk on Lake Joli Road the five miles to the nearest house with a telephone, and call a Bear River taxi from there.

As I began the walk, it started to snow heavily. By the time I reached the house, I was really beat. I had started walking at 9:00 in the morning and I arrived at 1:00 in the afternoon. It was not really a long walk but I'd had to lift my legs high over the new snow with each step. I could hardly lift my legs at all by the time I got to the house.

Finally, I got there, however. I was fed warm pie, and I was indeed able to call a taxi. The weather was turning ever colder. The taxi couldn't come out as far as the house, due to all the new snow, but it could get to the bridge in Morganville, only half a mile further on, to which I walked.

The driver who collected me at the Morganville bridge was Curt Rice. He got me to Digby in time for my appointment, and I arranged with him to take me back to the Lake Joli landing that same evening, where John was to meet me in the boat.

When we reached Bear River on the return journey, Curt stopped to change vehicles, and I was ushered into his special car. The front part of it all was engine. There was a seat for the driver and two additional small seats behind that one. The rest of the car was filled with bear traps, guns and all kinds of iron equipment, packed in, I supposed, for weight as well as utility, to keep the rear wheels from spinning on ice and snow.

We made it all the way to Lake Joli down the now icy and snow-laden road, but when we got there, we found that the lake itself had frozen. I wondered out loud how I was going to get across the lake and retrieve John.

Curt said, "I'll fix that."

We got out of Curt's car and walked down to the lake shore, and Curt went prodding around in the snowy bushes to find a canoe, which he did. People in those days didn't worry about other people stealing their boats and canoes, and they would just park them in the bushes near the landing.

Curt found a suitable canoe—perhaps it was his own—and we put it on the frozen lake. We got in and tried to pole it along over the ice, but that didn't work. A strong wind had blown the snow off the ice, leaving a clear black surface. We could get no grip on the slick new ice. The canoe just sat where it was.

"Well," Curt said, "I know one or two better than this."

There was a short rope, a painter, tied to the bow of the canoe, about five feet long. Curt said, "you sit there in the canoe, and I'll tow you over."

I said, "You'll what?!"

He said, "Don't argue with me, just sit there."

He took the rope in one hand, stepped carefully out of the canoe, and started to run across the lake, pulling the canoe along with me in it, his big, long legs flying. Every time he put his foot down, the ice cracked all around it, but he got that foot up and the next one down before the first step went through the ice.

He ran us between the point and the island, and then all the way across to the south shore. You could see the cracks in the ice he made with each step every bit of the way.

We walked up from the shore to the camp and found John working up on the roof. He looked down at us and said, "You're late for dinner."

He came down and we went into the cabin for some refreshment.

Soon Curt said, "Well, we'd better get back."

"How do you think we're going to do that?" I asked.

"The same way," he said.

I couldn't think of any counter arguments. We went down to the shore to look at the prospects. I was hoping the ice might have softened up and we could somehow break our way through it with boat or canoe, but no.

Curt took charge. Pointing to the canoe he said, "John sits there, and you sit there." John was greatly perturbed by this because it seemed to him beneath his dignity just to sit there like one of two helpless children, but there we were.

Curt picked up the canoe's rope and started running back across the lake, towing the canoe, now with two heavy passengers. He went east around the island this time, so he would not step on any of the cracks in the ice he had already made. The new route was nearly twice long as the first crossing. He ran the whole way, his great long legs just flying.

We walked up from the landing to where the cars were parked and Curt said, "I think we can get your car out of there."

I began to propose tying a rope to his car and to mine, but he said, "No. Get in there and get it started, and when I say give'r the gun, give'r the gun."

The car did start this time, but the back wheels just spun in place when I tried to drive it out of the snow onto the track of the road.

After the motor had warmed up, Curt got down in front of the car, picked up the front bumper and lifted the car up.

"Give'r her the gun," he said.

"I'll kill you," I said.

"Don't argue, give her the gun," he said.

So I gunned the engine and let out the clutch and—boom—the car sped out onto the road as he jumped aside.

"Well," Curt said, "I'm overdue in Bear River, so I'll leave you now."

He drove off and we followed.

We hadn't gone very far when I somehow got off the central crown of the road. The next thing I knew, the rear end had slithered around, and we were in the ditch.

Fortunately, Curt was still in sight and had been watching in his mirror. He stopped and backed up to us, and we went through the same performance a second time. "Give'r the gun!"

"I guess I'll stick with you until we get to Bear River," he said, "but I hope you won't mind if we stop at the old place. I've got some rabbits there I need to feed."

So, we stopped at the Sam Rice place, an old house and barn about half way out the Lake Joli Road. There was nobody living there at that time.

Curt had a bag of grain with him; it must have weighed 50 pounds. He tucked it under his arm and went to the barn. All around the floor of the barn were small basins.

He poured some of the grain into each one until the sack was empty. As he did so, he intoned, "Bunny, bunny, bunny; Bunny, bunny, bunny; Bunny, bunny, bunny."

Indeed, rabbits started coming out from wherever they had been hiding.

"They're fine rabbits," he said, and you could see they were, healthy-looking, large and numerous. "Bunny, bunny, bunny."

I asked him, "What do you keep them for? Do you raise them for their meat or their fur?"

He was shocked. "Meat!?" he exclaimed dismissively. "They're pets!"

Curt Rice's pets.

The Immigrant's Tale

My Irish grandfather, Archibald Ogilvie Leighton, was born in 1880 at Ballycarry, County Antrim, 16 miles from Belfast city along the north shore of Belfast Lough. His father, John Leighton, was a Scottish lawyer whose family traced its lineage back to about AD 800 and the arrival in long narrow ships of some Norse Løitens interested in real estate. They landed among the Picts in what is now the Lieutenancy of Angus and stayed for a thousand years, more or less. They were, variously, leather tanners and book binders, heroes and refugees, bishops and rogues.

They must have been story-tellers too, because their stories trickled along after them down the years.

~

One is of Robert Leighton, Archbishop of Glasgow (1670). On a voyage back from some business in London, he found himself in a storm more perilous than the ship's captain or crew ever had experienced. While the sailors wailed at their misfortune and the approach of certain death, the Archbishop walked the heaving decks seemingly without concern.

A sailor asked him how he could remain so calm in the face of his own imminent demise. He replied that they all were bearing witness now to the power and glory of God, and should this include his own death, then he would all the sooner join the heavenly host in the next world.

"But I do understand your terror," he told the sailor, "for I know where I shall be going, and you, you know where you will be going."

~

Love and opportunity brought John Leighton from Scotland to Ireland, and he settled in Ballycarry soon after he married my great-grandmother.

My grandfather Archie was the fifth of their eight children. His mother died when he was five and he was raised mostly by his elder siblings. His brother once taught him how safely to light a small firecracker that he had been given: you light it with the match and then you quickly throw it away. So, he lit the fuse and quickly threw the match away, and learned something about precision in language.

In all respects, his was a fine Irish childhood, and he ranged freely around the Antrim countryside from Carrickfergus to Whitehead and Islandmagee.

~

John Leighton is the only member of the family known to have stopped a train by shouting at it.

He expected his daily train to Belfast to depart the moment he stepped aboard, but not a moment sooner. His arrival at the train station was as precise as an atomic clock; but one day, as he crossed the foot bridge above the tracks to his train on the Belfast-bound side of the station, the train began to pull away.

His displeasure was immediate, and he bellowed out a commanding "Tut-dammit!"

The conductor heard, looked and pulled his signal rope. The train jerked to a halt. The engineer looked and backed up to the platform. John Leighton stepped aboard.

~

My grandfather became a structural engineer through apprentice-ship, and during this time he was sent here and there by his Belfast company to carry out tasks related to the trades of building construction.

One was to inspect the production and quality of building stones being quarried and cut by a supplier. He took a train south into County Down and then a sidecar to the quarry site.

At the gate, there was a short queue of men looking for work as day labourers. When my grandfather arrived, the foreman was speaking with one of these, a rather wiry middle-aged man, asking him if he really was physically suited to hauling heavy stones around on hand barrows, as the work required. The man did look a bit lean for such work. He also had a London accent, which made the foreman and everyone else highly suspicious of him.

The Londoner quietly gave assurances and the foreman finally shrugged and signed him on for the day.

The other workers were keen to make sport of the Londoner and he was paired as barrow-mate with the most massively strong and giant labourer among them. Several men had managed to place a very large stone on their barrow, and everyone watched as the hulk on the front handles sneeringly counted out, "One-two-three lift!"

To their disappointment, however, the wiry Londoner simply lifted up his end of the hand barrow and off they went with the stone.

For each subsequent load, some mean trick or other was attempted that might put the Londoner in his place, but none of them worked or seemed to disturb him. So it went, load after load, until they took a mid-morning break for tea.

The locals gathered together around a fire and a kettle, and left the Londoner to his own company. When the whistle blew and they reconvened at the rockface, they found a truly massive rock loaded on the Londoner's barrow.

His barrow-mate looked around at his fellows with anxious ferocity and shouted, "Who put that there?"

"I did," said the Londoner. He took hold of his two handles, and his hulking mate, with visible reluctance, took hold of his. "One-two-three lift," the Londoner said and lifted up his end.

Try as he might, his barrow-mate could not get his end off the ground. It was too heavy for him.

The locals were shamed, and just a little bit frightened, and there were no further tricks or nonsense for the Londoner.

My grandfather observed all this from the sidelines while checking the stone works. As he himself left the site at the end of the day, he found the Londoner standing near the entry gate, holding his day's pay.

"You're a great lifter," he said to him. "How do you manage it?" My grandfather was a very short and slight man, very unhappy with those two conditions, and no doubt anxious to learn from men like the Londoner, who seemed able to do so much with so little.

"I'm the weight-lifter in the circus that's set up in Downpatrick," he said, "but the company went bankrupt yesterday and they turned us all out. You can lift with brute strength or with technique. I use technique. I earned enough today to buy a ticket to Dublin. I've got some relatives there."

My grandfather gave the Londoner a lift to the train station.

~

About 300 years after the Løitens first arrived in Scotland, the Irish began making whiskey, invented it in fact, and in the mid 1800s Ireland produced the most and the best whiskeys in the world.

The best stuff came from the professional distilleries, but the artisanal versions, called poitin ('potcheen'), often were excellent, too. The quality of both took a deep dive to the bottom at the end of the 19th century, but in the 1890s and early 1900s, good poitin and bad poitin both could be found.

On one of his assignments as an apprentice engineer, my grandfather fancied some whiskey. He asked the local sidecar driver, whom he had been hiring to get around, if he could take him to a source of decent poitin, and after some cautious hesitation and a few coins, the driver said he could.

They drove deep into the countryside and, as they drove, the driver quizzed him at length about who he was and why he was in the area. Finally, they stopped at a farm gate and waited for the farmer to come out.

"Bill," the driver said, "the gentleman is wanting to buy some poitin."

Bill stood for a moment in deep contemplation of this information. "Poitin" he said. "Poitin, I have heard of it."

He thought a moment more and then pointed to the far horizon a few miles away. "Now, do you see there where the main road turns left and there's a wee side road to the right winding up over the crest of that hill? Well now, not at the first house, but at the third one on the left just over that crest, I've been told there's a man lives there could possibly guide you to some of what you are looking for."

"Och, Bill," the driver cut in. "He's just here working to build the new school. Sure, the gentleman's alright!"

"Oh, I see. I've got four gallons ready right now. How much would the gentlemen like?"

I never heard whether that poitin was good or bad.

Another time, he was sent to spend several weeks on Inishmore, the largest of the Aran Islands off the west coast of Ireland. It was an isolated place then, more or less as so wonderfully described by the writer J. M. Synge in his book *The Aran Isles*, which he completed in 1901.

There were few English-speakers on Inishmore, and not much for a young man to do. Every so often, the literati of the place (doctor, lawyer, undertaker, visiting magistrate, perhaps even Synge himself once in a while, and now my grandfather, as guest,) would gather at the priest's house, where they would talk and drink some Aran-made poitin brought by one or another of the participants.

That poitin unquestionably was terrible stuff, aged no more than a day or two but containing at least 50% potable alcohol all the same. As the poitin was passed around at these gatherings, the priest always would decline his share, apologizing that, because of his 'condition', he could only drink the poor substitute he had in a small bottle by his place at the table, a substitute which, nonetheless, he seemed to sip with enthusiasm.

During one such gathering, a visitor came to the door and the priest had to leave the room of revellers for a few minutes.

One of the revellers checked to see that the priest indeed was fully occupied and then quickly walked to the priest's place and took a small sip of his poitin substitute. He savoured it thoughtfully and then pronounced, "That's 10 years old!"

He passed around the priest's bottle for all to try and finished off the priest's own glass himself. He re-filled the glass and the now empty bottle with the rot-gut local brand and took his seat again.

When the priest returned, someone proposed a toast to their

good man of the cloth, who took such care of his flock, and all eyes were on the priest when he acknowledged the sentiment and then put his own glass to his lips.

There was a flicker, just a flicker, in those eyes at the moment of contact, just enough to show that the priest knew that his pretense to reserve his own good whiskey for himself was fully exposed.

My grandfather left Inishmore before he could evaluate the effect of this exposure on future revelry.

~

My grandfather's first job as a qualified structural engineer was building a new post office in Sligo town, with elegant, rounded bays and banded brick work. It was completed in 1901 and remains still a feature of the town.

While working there, he met and eventually married my grand-mother, née Gertrude Ann Hamilton, daughter of the grist miller in nearby Ballincar.

They emigrated to the United States in 1906. The plan was to go directly to San Francisco, where an earthquake had destroyed much of the city and a builder might be in high demand.

However, on the passenger liner in which they crossed the Atlantic, my grandfather met a Mr. A. D. Irwin of Philadelphia, and Mr. Irwin convinced him to come to Philadelphia instead of going west, and to join him in establishing a building business. This they did, as Irwin and Leighton, in 1909.

My grandfather quickly became a rich man. He worked hard and lived well.

~

My grandfather loved books, dogs and amusing himself and his friends.

His most memorable dog was Jock, a small terrier of great energy and, he claimed, of exceptional intelligence. As a convenience to himself, he had trained Jock to go and fetch for him the book he had most recently been reading. In this way, if he chose to read for a while in the garden after having read earlier in the day in his library, he could say to Jock, "Scoot." That was the signal to go and fetch the book he had been reading from wherever it was.

He used this trick with Jock to good effect at dinner parties. Before guests arrived, he would go to his library and select and look through a book suited to the occasion. At some appropriate point in the evening, he would bring the conversation around to the necessary topic, ancient Greek plays, for example, because *The Oresteia* was just then being performed in the city.

Then he might say, "*The Oresteia* is wonderful in its own way, but a bit boring, really, don't you think? I find Dikaiopolis in *The Acharnians* more interesting and amusing than I do old Agamemnon. Let me just read to you a few of my favourite of Dikaiopolis's lines. Jock, would you fetch me *The Acharnians,* that newest translation by Tyrrell. Off you go, scoot."

Jock would dash off and, to the amazement of all, would quickly return with precisely the requested book in his jaws.

~

Irwin and Leighton built hundreds of buildings all over the eastern United States, and this required my grandfather to travel to the many building sites, which he did mostly by train.

On one such trip in the 1920s, he went to the dining car for supper and was seated at a table at the far end of the car. From the menu, he selected the chicken pot pie but, being hungry and Irish, he added a side order of potatoes, offered on the menu as Lyonnaise potatoes: potatoes sliced and baked in butter. The dining car was full and the service slow; there was only one waiter.

Eventually, the chicken pot pie was brought to him, but no side dish of potatoes came with it. Twice he reminded the busy waiter about the missing potatoes, but still they did not arrive. The pie was cooling, so he waited no longer and ate it. His empty plate was whisked away and soon after his bill was delivered:

Chicken pot pie -	$2.00
Lyonnaise potatoes -	$0.50
Total -	$2.50

My grandfather tried several times, in an ever-louder voice, to get the waiter's attention and have his bill corrected, since he had never received the potatoes. By the time the waiter finally did respond to his call, all the diners in the car knew that the man at the farthest table had a complaint and my grandfather perceived that he had an audience.

He explained to the waiter that he never had received the potatoes and so the bill should be only $2.00, not $2.50.

The waiter was not having it. "No, sir," he said. "You don't understand. Those potatoes, they was *in* the pie." And he disappeared back into the kitchen.

My grandfather made no response, but soon rose, placed two dollars on his table, and walked slowly down the length of the dining car to the door.

The waiter scurried out of the kitchen to collect his money and then came hurrying down the aisle, speaking loudly as he approached. "Sir, there's a mistake here. Your bill was for two dollars and fifty cents, but you only left me two dollars."

My grandfather turned to the waiter, and also to the whole car of other diners. "The fifty cents?" he said. "It's *in* the two dollars."

~

My Irish/American grandparents immigrated one last time, to Nova Scotia and Digby County. It was at first an immigration of convenience. World War I prevented them making their usual visits to Ireland because ocean liners could not sail the Atlantic. At the same time, an epidemic of poliomyelitis was sweeping the eastern United States and travel to such normal summering places as the shores of New Jersey was prohibited.

It was a frightening time for families with children, all of them vulnerable to the terrible disease.

My grandfather asked his physician if there were any places in New England where polio was not present and where it would be safe to bring his family for the summer. His physician said there were not, but that there was an odd-shaped peninsula that jutted out from the nearby east coast of Canada that seemed to have been spared in the current epidemic.

My grandfather travelled by train to Boston and then by ship to Yarmouth, and hired a driver to take him looking for a suitable house to rent for the summer. Houses to rent were few then, and only when they arrived in Digby did he find one that would do, on Mount Street.

He sent for the rest of the family. My father, Alexander, was almost seven and his sister, Gertrude, just newly born.

My grandmother loved the Digby area. Physically, in many ways it resembled her home in County Sligo. Her Irish accent, which excluded her from Philadelphia high society, had no such effect here. Finally, they had found a place in North America where they actually felt at home.

Eventually, they bought a house on the Old Post Road in Smiths Cove, and later another down the hill on the shore, as a wedding present to my parents.

My father grew up roaming the fields and beaches and forests of Smiths Cove and Bear River, and he bonded to these completely as his home place. After the second World War, he managed to centre the major work of his career in Digby County.

He became a citizen of Canada and lived to the age of 99 years on the shores of Smiths Cove. He chose to die there, in the old Ben Hardy farm house he had rescued and rebuilt.

His children and grandchildren remain there still.

Kelsey Raymond's 1949 painting of the rebuilt Hardy house.

Bear Island.

The Emerald Isle

Bear Island is a defining feature of the Annapolis Basin, its Mont-St-Michel without monks or stonework. It is the view that we who live nearby take for granted, a narrow triangle pointing to the northwest with a wider base of sand and seaweed to the southeast, at the mouth of the Bear River. It is a green jewel on the landscape, 28 acres small and only a mile to walk around. It is a place where, now once again, nature has been left in charge.

The foundations of Bear Island were laid 500 million years ago, when it was a tiny piece of the massive continent of Gondwana, south of the equator. The red sandstone and slate shelves on which it now rests gradually pulled away from Africa and South America and, 200 million years later, collided with central Nova Scotia and Cape Breton. Seas arrived and disappeared, rose and fell and rose again until, not so long ago, a high bit of ground on the flooded floor of the Annapolis Valley became Bear Island.

My father first saw Bear Island when he was seven years old, and his family first came to Digby. From their house at the corner of First Avenue and Mount Street, he could walk one short block to Water Street and look east across the eel grass flats of that time and the Basin waters to the island, just off the Smiths Cove shore.

There was a house on the island then, in a grassy field, with a roadway down onto the beach, a home once supported by farming and fishing, but, by then, no longer occupied. The house was moved off the island not long afterward, into Smiths Cove village, where it remains today, a family home still, on the Old Post Road near the fire hall.

Relieved of the disruptions of human occupation, the island grew into a forest of tall white spruce and once again became a safe place for ground-nesting birds. In the 1950s, my parents took us there, for the adventure of it and for a picnic, once or twice each summer.

It is almost two miles from our home beach in Smiths Cove to the closest landing place on the island. Our small boat was heavily built of solid wood, too wide and awkward to row very far, and its ancient outboard motor weighed ten pounds per horsepower, of which it could deliver about five. Thus, our time on the island was always during a rising tide, so we would not have to drag the heavy boat down the beach to the water as the tide turned and went out again.

We always arrived, and mostly we stayed, on the beach of the island's western shore. The house had been on that side and once or twice we walked up where it had been and looked down into its well.

On those childhood visits, the main feature of the island was gulls. Herring gulls and great black-backed gulls, with nests and downy young, were everywhere, it seemed.

Mostly, we stayed close to the area of beach on which we landed, and tried to disturb the birds elsewhere as little as possible. However, I am sure we caused much harm when we visited during the nesting and rearing seasons of June and July.

When gulls in such a colony are frightened off their nests, their eggs quickly are broken and eaten, and their chicks killed in a mayhem of fear and predation. At the time, we didn't realize our visits could cause such damage. I know better now.

People must have first visited Bear Island only quite recently. As far as I know, no archaeological work has been carried out on the island itself, but people have lived in the Annapolis Valley for five or ten thousand years. Nature was abundant then and people were few. Bear Island may not have offered anything special to the people of that time, since the shores and waters of the Annapolis Basin everywhere must have been rich in foods and materials. If gulls nested on the island then, as they do now, for a few weeks each May, gulls' eggs would have been abundant and perhaps worth a visit to collect.

It seems most likely that the English name, Bear Island, comes from the island's location at the mouth of Bear River. One can imagine many possibilities for seeing bears along that river, leading to the name, but some insist that the name comes not from bears but from an early Acadian settler family named Hebert ('ay-bear').

Whatever the derivation, a bear or two must surely have visited the island over the past few millennia, but it is no place for a bear to live and they would have left as quickly as they arrived.

In the 1960s, some local sports decided the island would be a fine place to hunt rabbits and they loosed some snowshoe hares on the island, hoping they might become numerous. None survived, however. Then it was decided to sell the rights to the island's tall spruce timber and men arrived to do the cutting. To their chagrin, sand from the beaches had blown into the trees' bark, and it dulled their saws instantly.

Spruce beetles then were attracted to the island's uniform stand of mature spruce, and they killed nearly all the spruce trees. A few survived at the southeast end of the island and they or their progeny are still there today. A pair of bald eagles raised three eaglets in a nest in one of them in the summer of 2018.

However, over most of the island, the spruce forest has been replaced by a rich tangle of red elderberry, blackberry, tall mustards, goldenrods, and a hundred more grasses, forbs and shrubs, a richly-fertilized (by the birds), bushy, impenetrable, green carpet.

People use Bear Island still. Clam diggers frequent the tidal flats along the southeast sand bars. For about an hour at each low tide there is a land bridge to the island and occasional runners, horse riders and quad motorcycle drivers dash around the island on the beach and back again before the water rises and cuts off their escape for the next 11 hours.

These beach travellers do disturb the pairs of great black-backed gulls that nest on the beach above the high tide line. Most of the island's birds nest on the plateau above the beach, however, and probably are not much affected by these quick circumnavigators.

All of Bear Island except the southeastern sand spit is held in trust by the Town of Digby and its Board of Trade, and they have chosen to manage the island as a nature reserve, a local contribution to help buffer the current global crisis of plant and animal extinctions. Visitors are permitted, but must confine themselves to the beach, keep pets on leashes and under control, and stay off the vegetated plateau during the sensitive nesting season.

This is not a severe restriction. The brambles on the plateau are so thick that it is almost impossible to walk through them, and no one but the occasional visiting biologist would want to try.

Cormorants were rare in the Annapolis Basin in the early 1900s. Occasionally, my father or I would see one perched on a weir piling in Digby Gut. The weirs and the fish they once caught are gone now, but double-crested cormorants have returned. They probably were abundant here up to the 1500s, but they were killed and driven away by European colonists all across North America, followed by vast poisoning with DDT.

Use of DDT was phased out abruptly in the 1970s, and widespread persecution of wild birds was curtailed as well. Beginning in the mid-1970s, cormorants nested on Bear Island for the first time in living memory, in large, sturdy nests built among the branches of large bushes and in a few of the remaining trees. They have nested on the island ever since, with about 200 nests. They arrive from the south in April and depart southward again in October. In June and July, when they have young to feed, they often fish in St Mary's Bay, and fly back and forth over Conway in a constant flow.

I do not know if gulls nested on Bear Island when people lived and farmed there, but household dogs and cats and livestock probably would have kept them away. They have nested there ever since, however. I have always seen herring and great black-backed gulls nesting there in summer. The black-backs are the largest gulls and make nests along the beaches as well as on the plateau. Herring gulls now nest only on the plateau under cover of dense vegetation, perhaps to protect their eggs and young from predation by the black-backs.

It is hard to estimate numbers of nesting gulls in such places, but, based on the numbers of adult gulls that congregate on the island's shores in the spring, a reasonable guess is that there are 300-400 nests of each species on the island during the nesting season.

If you watch Bear Island from a nearby shore at dusk on a summer evening, you will see many great blue herons fly to it, arriving one or two at a time, from many different directions. They disappear into the darkening forest at the southeast end of the plateau, sometimes first alighting briefly on the island's shore before flying in among the trees. With so many herons arriving in the evening, you might think they were roosting together there or nesting in a colony, and you would be right.

About 40 pairs of great blue herons were nesting on Bear Island in the spring of 2018 when a quick spring survey was made. All of the nests were clustered in medium-height deciduous trees in the southeast zone of the plateau. The herons on Bear Island build their nests high off the ground but at heights at which the nests are nonetheless impossible to see from the beach or from a boat on the water.

No one knows for sure how many years the herons have nested on the island or how that number may have fluctuated over time. But in the last decade at least a substantial colony has nested there, and these birds fly out by day to animate shores and beaches all over the area.

One zone of the eroding outer bank of the island's plateau is perforated with small holes 2-3 inches wide and high above the beach. These are the nesting burrows of bank swallows. The burrows are newly constructed each spring and usually there are about 100 of them, of which perhaps 60 will contain active nests.

In 2013, the bank swallow was listed as a *Threatened* species by the Committee on the Status of Endangered Wildlife in Canada. It was estimated then that 98% of Canada's population of nesting bank swallows had disappeared since the 1970s. So, the nesting bank swallows on Bear Island are a national treasure.

Bank swallows were common in the Smiths Cove-Joggin Bridge area when my father grew up there in the 1920s. They still nested in the steep earthen bank near our family home in the 1950s and 60s, but then they did not return. There is plenty of nesting habitat there still, but no swallows.

Many factors are contributing to the bank swallow's demise. Preserving the places where they still nest, like Bear Island, seems especially important now.

Clearly, there are a lot of breeding birds on Bear Island in the summer. Each year is different. In 2019, for example, the gulls nested but then produced no young at all. However, on an average year, when the young of the year have fledged and adults and young are still together, there would be on the order of 900 cormorants, 2000 gulls, 200 herons and 300 bank swallows: 3400 colony-nesting birds, not including the Canada geese, sparrows, warblers, hummingbirds, sandpipers and plovers that breed on or otherwise make use of the island in summer.

Bear Island also is an island of seals. These days, they are grey seals, huge beasts with heads the size and shape of horses'. They arrive in early summer and depart in the fall.

They seem curious about intruders, closely approaching my small motorboat and craning their necks for a better view. On summer visits, I have seen five or ten, or none at all.

The grey seals are newcomers to Bear Island. I think I first saw them there in the late 1990s or early 2000s. The species is recovering from very low numbers due to shooting. This shooting was controlled and reduced in the early 1970s and recovery began shortly thereafter. Grey seals in the western North Atlantic are numerous once again.

Harbour seals were numerous on Bear Island in the late 1970s and 80s. They too were recovering from persecution and their numbers have rebounded. They are not often seen on Bear Island these days, however. Grey seals are large enough to eat them, and sometimes they do. Perhaps the Harbour Seals have moved to safer waters.

On my voyages around the island, I occasionally see one in the water close to shore or basking on top of a large rock made available by the receding tide.

You seldom see fish when visiting Bear Island. On summer days, sturgeon sometimes leap from the surrounding waters high into the air and fall back with a splash, and the occasional giant ocean sunfish, the *Mola*, waves a fin in the air while basking near the surface.

But fish there are. Unseen platoons of fish stream by the island, variously headed for survival, extinction or recovery as they navigate the habitat we have so radically changed for them. The salmon and herring and pollock and mackerel, still abundant in the mid-20th century, are mostly gone now; but eels and flounder, striped bass and smelt, shad and sturgeon surge past, persistent if not so numerous, and proof that nature is ever hopeful. In the 1950s, our neighbour Mary Stoddard caught a halibut in deep water just northeast of the island and my sister once found a fine, large lobster under a bed of rockweed on its shore.

Perhaps the island's now quite-barren shore one day will shake off the plastic debris of commercial fishing under which it now is buried and recover its former richness.

In winter, the birds that nested on the island in spring and summer drift away, the grey seals head for their winter colonies to give birth, and the island's plateau becomes a sleeping garden.

Its nearshore waters come to life, however. The ever-present common loons are joined by red-throated loons and red-necked grebes, and wintering ducks swell in number. Surf scoters, white-winged scoters, and black scoters join the buffleheads, long-tailed ducks, common eider, common goldeneye and Barrow's goldeneye, all diving to dine on periwinkles and green crabs.

They stay all winter, sustained by the bounty of invasive and native foods, sorting out as best they can their new ecologies. As winter softens into spring, they grow dazzling feathers, and their love songs echo along the island's shores until they depart for their northern breeding grounds.

Bear Island will not last forever. It is a mound of loose earth and sand rising maybe 30 feet above the water, eroded a little more by strong winds and tides every day. Eventually, it will become just another tidal flat in the Annapolis Basin.

If we fail to stop carbon emissions, sea levels will rise quickly and steeply, and Bear Island will as quickly disappear. However, if we save ourselves from this calamity, Bear Island too will be saved, and will be with us for a few more millennia.

Bear Island inspires us. It is a paradox of hope. Islands so close to peopled and touristed shores most often are lined with buildings, made into theme parks and glamping grounds, and become aesthetic plagues on the shared landscape from excesses of human enterprise.

Bear Island, however, has persisted as a rich piece of nature through all the thousands of years of local human co-existence. Its trees have been removed and its soils ploughed, its wildlife displaced or chased away as recently as the 20th century, but it has recovered and once again nourishes the entire region as a refuge and source of many elements of life and natural processes essential to us all, a natural dynamo in a depleted ocean, working out through experience what still is possible, holding for us the seeds of a replenished future.

John McGuire

When I first read *The Lord of the Rings*, in my teens, the only character I understood completely, right from the start, was Sam Gamgee. His personality and actions were totally familiar to me and none of the fantastic events of the story or its historical asides were needed to explain him.

Only recently did it occur to me that my familiarity with him was because Sam Gamgee had lived within and around my family from before I was born until I was sixteen. In the 1950s and early 1960s, our home was his garden and our family his charges, in need of much practical help and attention.

In those days, we didn't know him as Sam Gamgee, however. We knew him as John McGuire.

When I awoke each morning in Smiths Cove and looked out the window, John was likely to be in sight or sound, doing something. He arrived early, walking along the railway tracks the three quarters of a mile from his place to ours. He walked home for dinner and came back in the afternoon, and stayed until his work was done.

John was skilled in the use of the tools of rural living typical of the first half of the 20th century. He used a wooden wheelbarrow with a large metal wheel to move around everything he could not just carry himself. It was his constant helper and companion.

The grass around the house he cut with a scythe. Firewood he sectioned with a Swede saw, split with an axe and wheeled to the woodshed. He built sturdy small buildings but never used power tools.

In the forest, he always carried his double-bladed axe, one blade ground thin and sharp for chopping through tree trunks, the other ground to be wedge-shaped and less delicate, for cutting away the rock-hard bases of tree limbs and splitting firewood.

I especially remember John as my grandfather's yeoman and protector. My grandfather was Irish by birth and culture, and we grandchildren were taught to call him "Himself." I think John only ever called him Mr. Leighton. If there is a Frodo to be found in this account of John, he was my grandfather.

Despite social formalities and class awareness, a deep friendship developed between them, and when Himself would stay with us for a month each summer, John saw to his every need.

Himself's great pleasure was to fish for winter flounder at the outflow of the Joggin estuary, between Smiths Cove and Digby. For this, clams had to be dug for bait at low tide, and a heavy wooden rowboat had to be positioned on the beach where it would float up on the rising tide about two hours after the ebb tide had turned.

This required much hard pushing and pulling of the boat on big wooden rollers. The rollers had to be carried the 100 yards back up the beach and the oars, oarlocks and fishing gear had to be carried down to the boat.

When all was ready and the boat just afloat, John would row out, following Himself's precise directions, delivered from his seat at the stern. The course was defined by aligning the roof of the house, now at 188 West Old Post Road, with the roof of the main building for the rental cottages now at 234 Trunk Route #1. This line was followed northwest until the northern end of the gypsum storage shed at Deep Brook could be seen emerging from behind Jaggar's Point, which placed the boat eight-tenths of a mile off shore. There they anchored and began to fish.

On a good day, productive fishing lasted for an hour, sometimes two. Winter flounder surge hungrily into tidal feeding grounds following the incoming tide, and local knowledge of this behaviour informed John and Himself's fishing strategy. However, its strict dependence on the tides meant that, on some days, the right time to fish was inconveniently very early or very late in the day.

On those days, a different strategy was followed. A course straight north was set, defined by alignments of our own home's roof with that of the Winchester farm above Joggin Bridge, and it was pursued until the entire gypsum shed was visible across the southeastern sand spit of Bear Island, placing the boat a full mile from shore. Here the water was deeper, the tidal currents weaker and the flounder both less concerned about the state of the tide and less likely to be caught at all.

It never occurred to me to wonder how old John was. To me, he was an elder like Himself, but probably he was as much as ten years younger, born in about 1890. To me, John was physical strength and durability incarnate. He would lift and carry what no one else could or would. His waking hours were taken up with physical labour of some kind, never hurried or breathless, but constant.

The veins under the skin of his deeply-tanned arms were dark, turgid channels through which I imagined his blood flowed to give him his strength just as channels of steam powered the steam locomotives that pulled trains across our driveway several times each day.

John and Himself aged slowly together during my childhood, and they took care of each other in their own ways. In the early 1960s, they might sit together for a few hours near the beach instead of going fishing that day, exchanging stories and cigars.

The barn where we kept all the gear for boats and fishing was 200 yards from the beach and 15 yards higher in elevation. In

1957, Himself supervised the building of a two-story boathouse on a stone and earth platform just eight feet above the beach. It was his last piece of work as a structural engineer.

Thereafter, John no longer had to make the two or three round trips each day to the barn to fetch all the material for boats and fishing, and then to return them again. Instead, he had only to open the new boathouse doors and to close them again at the end of the day.

John never complained about his health, but he often wore a band of thick copper wire twisted around each of his wrists like a bracelet, a common folk remedy aimed at arthritis. My physician parents knew that, once long ago, John had suffered some kind of serious injury, and they took note of the copper bracelets. They were concerned that some of the work they might ask John to do could cause him pain or make his arthritis worse.

John was generally dismissive of such concerns, but one day my father was able to get him to talk about health matters. John admitted to some sore joints here and there, from old age he supposed. He wore the copper bracelets, but was quite sure they didn't do him any good. However, he had found a cure of sorts, that really seemed to help: a brand of waxy liniment formulated for lame horses.

"Where do you rub it on?" my father had asked, thinking the answer might show where John's arthritic pains were most severe.

"I don't rub it on," John said. "I take a big kitchen spoonful and melt it over a candle, and then drink it."

When I was eight or nine years old, I was allowed to visit John on my own at his home, usually on a Sunday when he was not working. It was a half mile walk along the Smiths Cove beach to the high bank upon which his small cabin was built, and then a long climb up the 20-foot wooden stairway he had built as a way down to the beach.

John never expected my visits but always welcomed me. He was a man of few words and always was soft-spoken, but he spoke to me as he would to a person of any age and made me feel very grown up. He would ask me about my life and tell me a little about his.

He would make us some real Maritime tea (two King Cole tea bags in each small mug, steeped *in situ* in boiled water for a few minutes and squeezed out into the mug, 25% of the tea then discarded to make room for copious evaporated milk from a can and two heaped spoons of sugar) and comment on whatever came to his mind.

John never told me his life's story. I only got a few un-connected vignettes that occurred to him to tell me for some reason. It seemed that as a young man he and a brother had travelled to western Canada and found work on the railroad. His brother had stayed but John had been injured and was dismissed from his job, so he had come back home to Smiths Cove.

John's sister, a Mrs. McGregor, lived in a house a few steps up the hill from John's cabin, at what is now 279 Trunk Route 1, and he had dinner with her most days. John also had a wife, apparently: one Stella McGuire, living somewhere in the village. He seemed to visit her occasionally, on a Sunday.

I do not recall ever meeting either Mrs. McGregor or Stella McGuire. Such adult relations did not interest me much in those days, and I never sorted out the what or the why of John's relationships. I could perceive in them some caring, some disappointment and some loneliness for him, but nothing more.

John's home was a framed one-room cabin with a window offering an unparalleled view out over the Annapolis Basin. It had a wood-burning kitchen range and maybe also a hot plate for summer. There was no telephone. He could receive news and messages through his sister.

The cabin I best remember was the second one he had built. It was a replacement for, and an improvement on, his first, which he had constructed upon his return from the west. Many would look on John's home as a small shack, but it was no such thing. In current lingo, it might better be called a "tiny home." John knew the meaning of "enough," and was content.

In 1963, my immediate family was away for the whole summer and Himself spent his time in Smiths Cove with John as his sole companion. He sent us news in letters, and one included what he called some recent "Johnisms."

John: "Are you coming back next year?"
Himself: "I don't know. I live from day to day."
John: "I live from hour to hour, a dollar an hour."

_____

John (while opening up some clams for bait while out fishing): "Herman Cossett showed me about half a bucket of clams he brought with him from the States and put in his fridge. Says they cost him three dollars."
Himself: "What's the matter with Herman that he can't dig his own clams? They are not too scarce this year."
John: "Stomach trouble."
Himself: "Ulcers?"
John: "Oversize. He can't stoop to dig clams."

In this letter, Himself included a sketch he had made, and introduced it as follows:

Hope you will like the little sketch below. A photo would

give a truer picture, but it would not put the necessary emphasis on John's suspenders, his peaked cap or the princess effect of his trousers. That is where the Art comes in.

"Land of hearts desire. Also John McGuire, the sea urchin, the grebe."

The sketch is the view looking east along the Smiths Cove beach from the walking path to the recently-built boat house, with its outside stairway to the upper floor. The *Sea Urchin* and the *Grebe* were our two wooden boats used for fishing.

Another Johnism was his insistence that the name *Grebe* (named after the bird) should be pronounced "greh-bee" and that the orange and yellow marigolds my mother liked so much and which he grew for her should be called "margolians."

Himself probably already knew he had cancer when he told John, above, that he lived from day to day. He died in the fall of 1964, and the last time I remember seeing John McGuire in Nova Scotia was at Himself's interment in our family cemetery in Smiths Cove in the summer of 1965.

John would not join us in the cemetery's small enclosure. He stayed alone, just outside its low stone wall, under a tree and partly hidden from us by branches. I think he truly was overcome with grief.

My family went its separate ways around 1965 and John soon left Smiths Cove. I learned about his leaving only after his departure, and so I never was able properly to say goodbye.

But John did not just disappear. He moved on to a new life. John's brother, with whom he had travelled west as a young man, had lived a good life there but recently had passed away in Winnipeg. His widow urged John to return out west for a visit and to stay as long as he liked. He went west and never returned.

I visited John in Winnipeg in the summer of 1973. I was 25 and was headed west myself for new adventures. I found John and his sister-in-law in a bright apartment half way up in a high-rise tower, looking east across the expanse of the growing city.

John was astonished but delighted to see me. He took me to each of the apartment's windows to show me the streets, the traffic, the faraway buildings, the excitement of modern construction that he

117

could watch every day. And there he was, loved and loving, cared for, smiling and joyful.

In response to a Christmas card a few years later, John's partner wrote to tell me that John himself had passed away a few months before. He must have been in his 80s then.

Like Sam Gamgee, John McGuire could hope and dream, but he also could create some happiness out of wherever he found himself and with whatever was at hand. This is the lesson I learned from John, his gift to me.

John never was called upon to carry the hope of the world up into the fires of a Mount Doom, but had my grandfather told John that he himself had such a job to do and needed his help, I am sure John would have loaded up his wheelbarrow with practical things and gone off with him. It is a wonderful thing to be able to find happiness in whatever you have, and carry on.

Kate Daily

The two-room school in Smiths Cove was our daily destination on winter days in the early 1950s. My sister and I would trek the long mile along the railway track to the school's door. In our classroom, there was a big pot-bellied wood stove just warming up for the day; rows of wooden desks for grades Primer, 1, 2 and 3; and our teacher, Mrs. Daily.

Mrs. Daily had grey hair and twinkly eyes, a large and perfect white handkerchief in her dress pocket, which she never used, a smile of warm encouragement, a leather strap, and a pet raccoon. The raccoon never came to school, but once we were allowed to visit it at her home.

Mrs. Daily had strict views about proper behaviour and encouraged us to meet her standards with both carrot and stick, but what a stick! The strap lurked in her desk or, sometimes, in that dress pocket. It was a thing to me so terrible that my heart stopped at each sighting, paralyzed by the notion of its possible application to me. A hangman's rope it seemed, a life-ending instrument made smooth and flexible, I was convinced, by use.

We trouped in on those wintry mornings, placed our coats and lunches on hooks and shelves at the back of the room, took our seats and soon were all busy at something, four grades of lessons made to happen, somehow, all at once, by teaching skills and methods perhaps now forgotten.

My seat in Primer was one row behind, and one to the left, of the much-venerated Duggy Woodman, in grade 2. Duggy was my friend Larry's big brother, and I felt especially important sitting so close to him. He was so big, so old, so important, a kingpin of our society. He sometimes grinned at me during class, and if he whispered comments to someone, I could hear them.

On this December day, Duggy had a terrible cold. Each breath he took made an admirable gurgling noise, somewhere between a purr and a growl. His eyes had a red and bulging prominence seldom achieved except by Hollywood makeup artists. His voice, when he feebly tried to speak, was a miracle of rasping utterances, squeaks, overtones and resonances inspiring in me an awe and astonishment only matched when, later in life, I heard a recording of a master Mongolian throat singer.

The impressive flows of lava from his nostrils were stemmed from time to time by heaving inward snorts of enormous sonorous complexity, beyond any possibility of effective imitation, and delivered unpredictably, so that each one was a thrilling surprise.

It was these heroic, powerful aspirations that caught Mrs. Daily's attention. "Douglas, there is no need to snort like a pig," she said, matter-of-factly. "Be considerate of others and use your handkerchief."

To my five-year-old ears, there was a take-no-prisoners tone in this admonition, a message that standards of decorum do not yield to mere physical discomfort, or might bring more. Somewhere deep inside Mrs. Daily's desk, the leather strap twitched.

Mrs. Daily stood straight and solid beside her desk, staring down the rows, her position on pig-like snorts impossible to misinterpret, even by a pet raccoon. Her clarity and confidence brought to my mind a story about my great grandfather.

My parents told us stories, and they fell on impressionable ears. One of my favourites was about the year my great grandfather Hamilton had spent in Upper Canada in the mid-1800s. Perhaps he should have stayed there. Everything else I ever heard about him seemed a bit sad: the grist miller at Ballincar, County Sligo; hard working, henpecked, deprecated by wife and family seemingly because he enjoyed a pint with friends more than church.

But he came to rural Canada as a young man to visit a married sister who had homesteaded there, and to have some adventures before taking up his adult destiny as the miller in Ireland.

Upon arrival, he learned that the teacher in the local grade school had just been thrown out of the window by his students, and had left the district, as had several predecessors. Teachers were not plentiful then. Many a 16- or 18-year old might, technically speaking, still be in grade 3 for lack of opportunity for advancement. The district needed a new teacher, and my great grandfather apparently needed a job, so he signed on with the local school board and took aim at discipline.

When he entered the school on his first day, all the students, including the bearded members of grade 3, were there, eager to meet their new object for sport and intimidation. He went straight to his desk at the front of the class and took from a bag he was carrying an 18" steel spike and a large hammer. He then strode to the school's entry door at the back of the room, stood on a chair, and pounded the spike into the wall above the door frame far enough that it was firmly affixed.

He marched back to his desk and took from the same bag a large revolver and a box of ammunition. He loaded all six chambers, sat down at his desk, steadied his elbows and grip on the gun, and proceeded to drive the stake into the wall with 12 well placed shots, Bam! Bam! Bam! Bam!—loading his gun midway through the demonstration.

At the end, as the smoke cleared, he loaded the gun again, put it in his desk drawer and said, "Now, class, let's begin, shall we?"

That pleasing vision faded, and I quickly was brought back to the very present Mrs. Daily. Duggy was on dangerous ground. Resist it though he tried, a tide of mucus and misery was rising within him. His respiratory purr now sounded more like drowning. His muted sniffles were bringing no relief and then, before my riveted eyes, he stopped breathing. His face became deep red, then blue, then black, like the clouds of an October hurricane.

His chest and shoulders began to heave in a slow rhythm of great inward gasps. With each gasp, he leaned forward then back, and as he did so, to my delight, a mass, exquisite in size and form, bulged from his left nostril with each forward swing, a little farther each time, a millimetre, a centimetre, an inch: Ah...ahhh...aaahhh-hhh...

Duggy discharged an Olympian sneeze, a gold medal among sneezes. All pretense of control was relinquished, and from his throat there came a shout and a howl so powerful that sparks showered onto the floor from the air vent of the pot-bellied stove and an eraser fell off the blackboard ledge.

But what made the sneeze truly extraordinary was the marvellous massive torpedo that shot straight out of Duggy's left nostril. It had the mass and momentum of a lead slug suited to hunting bears, a thing of spectacular size and weight, and it hit the floor right in the middle of the aisle with a thud and splatter I can still feel to this day. The mess on the floor remained connected to Duggy's left nostril by a thick tentacle of shining slime at least three feet long that seemed to have the strength and substance of a space-age glue.

At that instant, as if in a reflex of recovery and survival, Duggy gave a snort more terrific than any pig could ever hope to utter, a ripping, ululating, roaring aspiration as if the oxygen in that breath would save his life or nothing could.

And at that same instant, the normal laws of physics seemed to have been suspended. Perhaps the earth ceased its normal rotation and gravity ended for just that moment. However nature may have conspired to make it possible, it was surely an epic moment in the history of humankind.

For as Duggy's massive snort developed full power, that three-foot rope of miracle slime went tight, the medusa on the floor co-alesced, and the whole great shiny mass shot straight back into Duggy's left nostril, like the tongue of a frog having retrieved a distant fly.

The impact knocked him against the back of his chair, where he slumped, dazed and exhausted, a thin patina of floor dust decorating his face. The shiny iridescent torpedo re-entered its bay and protruded again with a pulsing menace, as if ready for a second shot.

My eyes swam with admiration. Who else had seen this miracle? Surely, Duggy must be a saint. I wanted to leap up, to call for general applause, for celebration, to bear witness to this singular event for all of time.

But my elation was cut short. There was another important witness.

Mrs. Daily was glowering down the very aisle where the miracle had just taken place, and she did not seem impressed or moved in any way. "Douglas Woodman!" she exclaimed and began to approach Duggy with a steady measured step, staring straight at him. There was no smile of admiration or amazement, no smile at all. She was advancing on Duggy one un-hurried step after another, and she was reaching into her pocket.

"Here," she said. From her pocket she pulled out that big, white, perfect handkerchief she always carried but never used, and gently but firmly wiped Duggy's face and nose with it. "Keep this," she said. "I'll take you home at recess."

Maggie Morine

It was right here where I first seen the cougar, not out on the other road like I told Millie and Randy. I come to this place a lot, except in winter and hunting season, mostly on my way home from night shift at the fish plant.

It's some nice here in the early morning. It's real easy to get to, but seems don't nobody come here but me. You can't see it from the road, that's probably why, and there's no path to it; you have to find your own way down.

I first come here one spring lookin' for fiddleheads, following this tiny brook you can hardly see where it flows under the road. I never found no fiddleheads, but I found this little waterfall bubblin' into a pool just a short way along. This big smooth rock by the pool is where I like to sit and let my work shift just slip away, that last frozen lobster popped out of its shell and into the bin.

They're kilt quick and painless now, them lobsters are, no more boilin' alive. I like that part.

Mostly what I hear at this pool is the brook and the birds. My land! There's some birds here in May, singin' or shoutin' or whatever it is they do! It's like the brook and the birds is having some kind of big conversation. I just listen; it's so musical.

I think that cougar must'a saw me a good few times before I ever saw her. The way she can just melt away into the bushes and disappear, I'd only ever see her if she wanted me to.

But one time I looked up and there she was, just across the little pool, standin' sideways and lookin' at me. I was some scared! I guess I'd seen a few on TV, but not like this; the size of her!

She must'a seen how scared I was. I remember she looked at me for a while, then she looked away, and then she looked back at me again the way you look someone right in the eye. Then she just twitched her tail and walked away into the woods.

We got kind of acquainted after a while. She never come close, but she often come out to the pool when I was there.

One day I asked her if I could snap her picture; funny I felt I had to ask! She didn't seem to mind.

I got one of her sittin' lookin' at the brook where it flows out of the pool and then, just when I snapped a second one, she jumped right over the brook to the other side. What a picture I got! She's right up in the air, all four paws off the ground, legs stretched way out front and back, tail in a long straight line, the brook bubblin' underneath her.

I got a print made of that one and I keep it in a special place, along with a few little tufts of her hair I found once on the blackberry thorns.

I probably shouldn't'a showed that picture to Phyllis. I knew she would love the beauty of it, and she did, but she's a generous person that don't like to keep nice things to herself, and she's always doin' stuff on her phone.

One afternoon when I was just getting' up, my sister Annie come burstin' in with the city newspaper sayin', "Maggie, you're famous," 'cause I was on page seven, or at least my picture of the cougar was.

Someone named Millicent Lafever was writin' that a real, live cougar had been discovered, roamin' wild, right here, right now, in southwest Nova Scotia. She must'a seen my photo somewhere and maybe tracked down Phyllis. Millie said there was cougars seen in the province before, but every time, the Wildlife said the reports was mistaken and false. With my picture, Millie was sure there could be no doubt this time.

Annie said I should feel proud and important for the big discovery.

Next afternoon, Annie come burstin' in with the paper again. Now the cougar story was on page 3, but the story was different. It said that Chief Wildlife Officer Randolph Nix had studied my picture in some special way and found it was all fake, just a photo of a plain old cat doctored up to look like a cougar and put on a phony background. Anyone with a computer could do that, he said. Accordin' to him, there weren't no cougars in this province, never had been, never would be. He said it was wrong to go makin' up such stories.

I was just enjoying my last hour of sleep the next afternoon when that Millie Lafever herself come knockin' at the door, all the way down here from the city. She was some riled up. She figured Randy Nix had called her a liar and a fool right in her own newspaper and she was gonna make him eat his words.

She asked me if I had that picture still on my camera, and she took it straight onto her computer, so she'd have the real thing. She asked if I had any pictures of the cougar's tracks or anything else and I said I had one little tuft of her hair.

That really fired Millie up and she just begged me for it, sayin' it could probably prove everything.

She asked me to show her exactly where I'd seen the cougar and I said I would, but I didn't. I took her on a different road to another spot with another little brook and a big patch of blackberry brambles. She checked where she was on her phone, thanked me, and zoomed away.

It was about two weeks later when Annie come burstin' in on me with the paper again. Millie had an article right on page 2, sayin' that the paper's photo experts had decided my picture was real and that some scientists had tested the hair and it was 100% cougar and a female, at that.

She said it was me, Maggie Morine, who'd finally proved there was cougars in the province. She had some bad things to say about Chief Officer Randy denyin' the truth just because a cougar is inconvenient to his line of work. She sounded pretty pleased with herself.

I finally met Randy a few days later, when I'd stayed at the plant one morning to do an extra shift. The boss pulled me off the line and said there was Wildlife guys in the plant office wantin' to see me.

There was Randy, acting like he had to be polite but not really feeling that way. He wanted everything I had about the cougar, and he wanted it now.

The boss told me they could manage without me for the rest of the shift, and I had best just go get the officers what they wanted.

Randy asked me all the same questions as Millie. He took my camera away and said I'd get it back later. He told me to take them right to the spot where I seen the cougar, so I took them to the same place I took Millie. Randy said they were going to set up cameras and bring in some tracking dogs and find out for sure if there really was a cougar around.

On Sunday I finally saw Phyllis after not seein' her for quite a spell. She said the cougar thing was just crazy on Facebook. There was people wantin' to know right where it was seen so they could go shoot it to prove it was there, and others who wanted it shot so it would be safe to walk in the woods again.

Others was sayin' that there should be special new laws to protect cougars and that the hunting season for deer should be closed to be sure none got killed by accident. About half was sayin' the Minister should arrange to hunt down that cat and make people safe again and the other half was tellin' the Minister to close the woods to save the cougars.

A few days later, Annie come burstin' in with the paper again. Right on the front page was the Wildlife Minister declaring that the facts were all in and that there was no cougar in the province. Everyone could relax and forget about it.

On page 5 there were opinions by Randy and by Millie, side by side. Randy was explaining how the lab test on the hair couldn't be trusted and the photo was too poor to use for identification. The dogs and cameras had found nothing. Millie was saying that the Wildlife Branch was just denying facts they didn't want to deal with and that the Minister should be ashamed for lying to the people.

About two months later, I got my camera back in the mail. It still worked fine, but my cougar pictures were gone.

That's about the time I come back to this little pool again. I'd stayed away ever since my picture got into the paper just to keep it out of harm's way. I'll never bring my camera here again; I've learned that lesson!

I did bring that last newspaper article, though, and when the cougar showed up the next time, I read to her what the Minister had said about her not being around. For her, I figured it was the best kind of news.

And me, I don't really care how much Millie or Randy want to be right. They can go lookin' for cougars themselves if they really want to.

I figure you'll meet cougars if you go to the right places, and stay long enough for them to find you.

The cougar.

Ted and Alec Leighton

Reet Crocker

A play in one act

For my Newfoundland mentors: Con O'Brien (1916–1997), Joe O'Brien (1925-1995) and Victor Williams (born 1930), all of Bay Bulls.

The Setting:

The interior of a root cellar, a well-like hole in the ground made to store vegetables. It is summer in Halloran Harbour, a fictional small village on an island off the south coast of Newfoundland. Halloran Harbour is in the process of deciding to accept or not a government-sponsored resettlement of its residents to the mainland, anywhere they might choose to relocate.

The cellar is a cylindrical excavation, about 15 feet in diameter, dug into the ground such that the floor is about 8 feet below the inner ceiling. This ceiling is overlain with soil and thick sod, about one foot thick, above the roof timber supports. That sod is continuous with the grassy ground into which the cellar originally was dug.

The cellar has been superficially re-purposed as Reet Crocker's dwelling. It is seen as a cut-away section which removes the half of the cellar's wall toward the audience. The floor space of the cellar extends downstage toward the audience to provide more space for players and props.

The floor is of packed earth overlain with rugs. The walls of the cellar are of rough stone mortared together and embedded in the surrounding earth. The roof slopes upward 15-20 degrees from the top of the cellar's stone wall to a centre point and the roof protrudes as a smooth hummock in the surface of the surrounding unmowed grassy level ground, seen in profile high above the stage surface.

Actors come to and go from the cellar from one side of the stage across a walkway that is perceived by the audience as a path across the surrounding grassy ground. On the upstage side of this path to the cellar, near the cellar's entryway, there is a small solar panel about 1 foot square mounted about 3 feet off the ground on a post that extends another 2 feet higher still and has, affixed to its top, an antenna that might serve for AM-FM radio reception.

The scene design should include details of the grassy ground above the cellar that indicate high summer—tall grass still quite green but mature, some wildflowers, etc. Lighting should show the above-ground area on a bright sunny day.

The entrance to the cellar is built like a small ship's companionway. It is at centre stage and level with the back wall of the cellar, and it opens to a vertical ladder descending straight down along the back wall.

There are no windows and no natural light in the cellar. Light is provided by two kerosene-burning lamps with simple single wicks and glass chimneys. The stage lighting will suggest the warm colour tone and dim light of the oil lamps but need not mimic the actual direction and dimness of the light that would come from these two weak lamps. Tiers of shelves originally intended to hold potatoes and other winter vegetables cover the walls up to about 6 feet in height, with the shelves 1-2 feet apart vertically. There is a space for the ladder through this semicircle of shelves.

A section of one of the lowest shelves off to one side is made up as a bed, or painted to portray one, resembling a small ship's bunk bed for crew members. There is a small bedside table off to one side, and a second small but larger table with two chairs.

On the larger table is a modern one-burner butane cooking stove as might be used for camping or in restaurants for on-table cooking. Not far from the stove, attached to the edge of the highest shelf, is a modern-looking smoke/carbon-monoxide alarm. There is a small radio on the bedside table and two wires, loosely twisted together, descend from the ceiling nearby, with loose attachments to the shelves, and are attached to the radio (from solar panel and antenna). The furniture can extend down-stage as needed. There are tidy stacks and piles of all the material needs of very simple living on the shelves.

Credits: In whatever form the names of the actors and other credits for the performance are provided to the audience, this information should include the following statement:

"Fiddle tune: *I Buried My Wife and Danced on Top of Her*. Traditional Irish"

Characters

Rita Crocker ("Reet") – the inhabitant of the root cellar, age about 70. Reet dresses very casually, simply and for warmth, with a long dull skirt over thick woollen leggings, blouse, thick sweater, heavy socks, thick slippers. Her hair is grey, shoulder length, brushed but not especially groomed, tied back. She wears knitted gloves with the finger portions 2/3 cut away so that half the length of her fingers is bare. No makeup. Face and hands clean.

Dora – Reet's daughter, in her 40s. Modern (2020s), modest but new and well-fitted clothing, hair styled, dyed, groomed. Simple jewellery and makeup.

<u>Mary Moores</u> – A radio show host in St John's (NF). Late 20s, attractive, well-groomed and well-dressed but in a casual-professional way: pants, blouse and light dress jacket under a heavy coat appropriate for a two-hour crossing over cold ocean waters in a small open boat. She carries a small briefcase with a shoulder strap.

Scene 1 – 10 am

> *LIGHTS UP to reveal REET sitting at her kitchen table, play-*
> *ing 'I Buried my Wife and Danced on Top of Her' on a fiddle,*
> *slowly, rhythmically, competently.*
>   *A kettle is heating on the butane burner on the table, and*
> *everything is laid out to make tea for two. The lamps are lit*
> *inside the cellar, and outside it is full daylight. There is an*
> *opened can of evaporated milk and a sugar bowl on the*
> *table, at the ready.*
>   *DORA, wearing a warm jacket and outdoor shoes and*
> *clothes, ENTERS and crosses to the companionway, opens the*
> *door, and leans into the opening.*

DORA
Good morning, Mum. I'm coming down.

REET
(happily) Dora, dear! Watch your step now. I'm making us some
tea.
(Putting the fiddle on a shelf.)
 Just leave that door open. It's nice to have the bit of sunlight.

> *Dora steps through the companionway onto the ladder and*
> *descends.*

REET
How's your cousin Francie today?

DORA

She's okay, I think, but it's a hard time for her just now. Our family and Frank's are doing a lot for her, but Frank's away working most of the time, and now, without Auntie Bea, she's a bit overwhelmed.

> *Finally down the ladder, she give Reet an affectionate kiss.*
> *She leaves her coat on, pulls out a pair of knitted gloves, and*
> *puts them on.*

REET

(making tea)

My sister's probably glad she's dead and gone now, dead before all this resettlement stuff has finally come to a head. Now at least she doesn't have to vote the Harbour into oblivion, which the rest of us likely will.

DORA

(sitting at the table)

Frankie loved your birthday present, Mum. Was that book from the old school library? He loves the poems and the fish. Look, he made you this thank-you card.

> *From a pocket, Dora produces an 8.5 x 11-inch piece of plain*
> *white paper with a big heart on it drawn crudely in thick red*
> *crayon, as by a 6-year old. Above the heart is awkwardly*
> *printed "Auntie Rita" and under the heart is printed*
> *"Frankie", in crayon of different colours.*
> *Reet takes and inspects the card.*

REET
"Auntie Rita; from Frankie."
(short, warm laugh)
Little Frankie! - Francie, Frank and Frankie, lots of Fs in that family.
Bea laughed and laughed when Francie told her they'd named the
baby "Frankie."

  I got no fridge to stick this to, but I can put it right here.

> *Finds a thumbtack and attaches the card to the shelving near*
> *the kitchen table, then pours tea. She sits at the table during*
> *the following and they sip as they talk.*

REET
What are people saying these days about the vote, Dora? I haven't
been out for a while, not since the day you arrived. Anyone still
serious about staying put?

DORA
It's tearing some families apart, Mum. It's an awful thing, really.
Some can imagine living away from the Harbour and some just
can't. I expect most will go for resettlement, but it's hard to say.

REET
Maybe you youngsters should take some of we old nay-sayers out
in a boat and just throw us overboard, be sure of a good majority
vote for the leave side.

DORA
(assured tone)
I know how you'll vote. We've got the apartment all ready for you.
Eddy and Jeanie go in there every day now and play Grandma-
Rita's-coming-to-live-here games.

REET
I hope they'll call me Grandma Reet! What about Armand? Is he waiting eagerly too?

DORA
You know he thinks you're wonderful, Mum. He doesn't understand why you've spent the last four years living in this root cellar, but I guess no one else does, either. He's delighted you're moving in with us. He thinks you'll fit right in, and you'll give us some real family close by. We've missed that this long while.

REET
I'm after being on this island all my life, Dora, except six months at Normal School. Seventy years. Do you really think I'll survive a move to Halifax?

DORA
I did, Mum. You can too, and you will. There's a pub full of fiddlers just down the street from us can't wait for you to join them, and the libraries need volunteers something bad.

> *Reet chuckles at the thought of waiting fiddlers and needy libraries.*

REET
Well, we've got to wait two days for the big meeting and the vote. I don't even know if I'll go to it.

DORA
You're famous this week, you know, Mum. You're all over Facebook! And now the radio's after you. Joey Frampton said he brought Mary Moores over this morning in his skiff—Mary Moores her own

self, from the CBC! She told him she's come to interview you!

REET
How does this happen Dora? I hear Mary talking on the radio every morning. She's a daily comfort and like a movie star to me, but from some other, far-away world. Two days ago, she up and phones Myrtle at the post office, sent Ferdie over to ask me would I be interviewed! She's coming here this afternoon at two o'clock, all the way from St. Johns. Why does she want to talk to me?

DORA
One of those government people took a picture of your cellar with its antenna and solar panel and ship's companionway for a door, with the land sloping down to the sea in the background. It's a lovely photo, Mum. It must have struck him as funny and quaint, a ships cuddy buried on a rise of land in an old garden by the sea. He put it up on Facebook and wrote "Halloran Harbour, where an elderly lady lives in a Hobbit Hole." It got re-posted all over the place. Armand says it had 400,000 views, last time he looked.

REET
Lord Jesus! There must be a few other planets out there, different from the one I live on.

DORA
Mary seems like a nice person on the radio. You'll have fun talking to her, I know you will. She'll have to watch out or you'll end up interviewing her, if I know you! Just don't tell her anything you don't want the whole universe to know.
(Standing)
Gotta go, Mum. Francie needs my help with baking. Everyone's so stirred up about the vote, they're visiting all over all the time, just

talking and worrying; it's tea and cakes nonstop, and she still has to home-school Frankie.

REET
Maybe we need some mummers goin' round right now, squeezing the reticent for their opinions and making a party of it.

DORA
Mummers scare people into speaking the truths no one wants to hear, Mum. Leaving the Harbour after 300 years of living here is terror enough.

REET
(to herself)
Yes, we've had terror enough.

DORA
Will you come to supper tonight? You will, won't you? It'll be a proper jigs dinner. We want to hear about that interview, and Frankie's been asking for you.

REET
(snapping back from being lost in thought)
Yes, for sure I'll come.

Dora takes one step up the ladder; pauses.

DORA
They're still looking for Dad, Mum. The police come by the house every few months to keep me posted. They came again last week. They think he might be out on the street in a city somewhere, even though it was here in the Harbour he disappeared.

REET

No one's seen Dermot for almost two years, as far as I ever heard. The police used to come all the way out here to tell me they were still looking, but I told them to stop; if they hadn't found him yet then they never would. I moved in here to finally be quit of him. I told him if he ever tried to come down that ladder, I'd chase him out with this.

> *Reet brandishes a fish fork with a five-foot handle and two long sharp tines.*

REET

Time and again he'd leave the Harbour for a while and then come back, for 25 years, and each time he come back he was worse than the time before. After I moved in here, he must of just took off for good.

> *Dora steps back down and takes her mother's hands.*

DORA

I know it was awful, Mum. You saved me from the bad side of Dad; you sent me away to school and I never came back. I never had to suffer any of what you did.

REET
(tossing off the dark thoughts)
Well, he won't be waiting for me in here tonight when I come back from supper with you and Francie and Frankie, and come I will.

> *Dora kisses Reet, then nimbly climbs the ladder, goes out the companionway, and EXITS, removing her gloves as she goes. After watching her to the top of the ladder, Reet clears the*

table and heats water to wash dishes. She pauses, deep in thought, then reaches for her fiddle, tucks it under her chin, pauses for a moment more, and then, with a short, quiet, ironic half laugh, half sigh, she begins playing the same tune.

FADE TO BLACK

Scene 2 - later

LIGHTS UP. Reet is brushing and tidying her hair. The table is again set for tea for two. The water is heating.
     MARY MOORES ENTERS, crosses purposefully to the open companionway. She leans into it.

MARY
Mrs. Crocker?

REET
(enthusiastically)
Hello, Mary! I'd know your voice anywhere! Please come in.

Mary starts down the ladder.

REET
 Just watch your step.

Once down, Mary shakes Reet's hand formally but warmly.

MARY

Mrs. Cocker, I'm so glad to meet you. As you know, I'm Mary Moores from CBC Radio in St John's. Thanks so much for agreeing to speak with me and to let me visit your home.

She starts to take off her coat.

REET

You'd best leave your coat on, Mary. Not that I want you to be leaving anytime soon. It's about 50 degrees down here all the time; I guess that's about 10 degrees these days. Here, put these on, too.

Reet hands Mary some thin knitted gloves.

REET

You'll be more comfortable with these. Please, sit down here. I'm just making us some tea. You'll have some, won't you?

While Reet makes and pours tea, Mary sits, places her briefcase on the floor and takes from it a small microphone on a cable and a small voice recorder. She sets these on the table, plugs them together and places the microphone on a small table-top stand. Mary looks around the cellar carefully, taking it all in as best she can. Reet puts two cups of tea on the table and sits.

MARY

Shall we begin?

Reet nods.
Mary switches on the recorder.

MARY
(professionally)
I am here today with Mrs. Rita Crocker at her home in Halloran Harbour, on the south coast of Newfoundland. Many of you will know Mrs. Crocker as the recent 'Facebook phenom' who lives alone in a root cellar, or maybe it's a Hobbit hole, in this remote island community. Good afternoon, Mrs. Crocker!

REET
(also professionally, taking up her role)
Good afternoon, Mary, and please call me 'Reet,' or I won't know who you're talking to. Welcome to the Harbour.

MARY
So, Rita—

REET
'Reet', please.

MARY
Oh, yes...So, *Reet*, I want to talk about your home in this root cellar, but first tell me about Halloran Harbour and your life here. I understand you have lived here for a long time.

REET
Indeed I have, Mary. This was the root cellar for the house I was born in, in 1950, and I've lived in the Harbour ever since. When I was 17, I spent six months in St John's at Normal School and when I came back, well, pretty soon I was the schoolteacher. I taught school here for 35 years, until they closed the school and pensioned me off. There were hardly any kids left by then.

MARY

That lovely frame house I walked past to come to this cellar, was that your family home?

REET

My great-great grandpa built that house, around 1865. Seamus Maloney he was, a starveling from Ireland, from County Cork somewhere. But he and his family did well here in the fishery; I guess they knew a thing or two about making up salt fish. We were well-to-do by local standards, until my generation. That's how I could go away to school; most could never afford it.

MARY

You must have seen a lot of changes here over all those years.

REET

Mostly for the worse, Mary, at least in my lifetime. The market for salt fish fell right off and the new buyers of fresh fish were too far away to get to. Then the salmon disappeared, then the cod disappeared. Now there's hardly a capelin comes in to spawn. But some things got better. We got a nursing station and a bit of money for the school. In the 70s we got electricity and a bit of telecommunication, although don't bother trying to use your cell phone here. If someone gets really sick or hurt, a helicopter will come. But there's no work here now; people have to ship away to the mainland or to Canada to earn a living. More and more never come home again.

MARY

I met your daughter today. She saw me walking around the village and invited me in; I guess she knew I was waiting to come see you. Tell me about your family, Reet.

REET
We're all one big family here in the Harbour, in a way. If we ever
had a telephone book, you'd see that we're nearly all Maloneys and
the rest of us are Crockers: Irishmen and west-country English-
men. But there's been plenty of coming and going, too. We're a hale
and hearty crowd, and not so closely related as you'd think from
the names.

MARY
Has your daughter lived here all her life, too?

REET
Indeed, she has not. She boarded out on the mainland for high
school and then went on to university. She married a man from
Corner Brook and they both got work in Nova Scotia. Now she runs
the whole computer system up there.

MARY
Was your husband from a different community, too, like hers?

REET
No, my dear. He and I were toddlers and school kids and teenagers
together right here. Dermot Crocker came from the finest line of
the Crockers. They had the best boats and the best cod traps and
t'was the merchant owed <u>them</u> money. Every man of them could
haul a Hood family; I guess that doesn't mean anything now, but
it's strong they were, and clever and wise, and they made sure
there was some fun in life in good times and in bad. It was
Dermot's grandfather taught me the fiddle. Dermot played accordion and the two of us kept the whole Harbour dancing!

MARY
But your husband's no longer with you?

REET
Poor Dermot, no. Life was hard on him after a while. He was a fish-
erman through and through, but by the time he was 40, the fishery
had fallen apart, and he fell apart with it. He was like a captain of a
grand clipper ship when the steamboats took it all over. Many a
time he went away looking for work, but his spirit was broken.
Every time he came home, he was just more hopeless, and sad and
vexed with the world. He went away for the last time nearly two
years ago. No one's seen or heard from him since.

MARY
What a terrible distress that must be for you, your husband just
disappearing without a trace.

REET
(With a mix of intensity and wistfulness) It was hard when he was
at home and sad and angry, and it's hard now when he's gone.

MARY
Your daughter Dora told me that you have been living in this cellar
for four years. Can you tell me what brought you here?

REET
(after a slight pause)
I set this place up to be a little sanctuary for myself, where I could
play music and read—and listen to CBC Radio—without annoying
poor Dermot when he was at home. Then, when he would go away,
I felt less alone in here than in our big empty house, so I decided to
live here. It's kind of like living in a ship, you know, like in the

cuddy of one of those small schooners used to trade everything here before Confederation.

MARY
Well, four years is a good long stretch; you must have made yourself comfortable here.

Short pause.

MARY
Where did your husband go after he left here?

REET
That's a mystery to everyone, Mary. When he went away before, he always sent some word to me or to his brother, usually needing money, but at least we knew where he was to. We've heard nothing now for almost two years. The police say they keep looking for him through some kind of network they have, but they haven't found him.

MARY
Do you have any thoughts yourself, about where he might be?

REET
I don't know what to think. No one here knows where he went, or even how or when he left the Harbour. His family and the police checked all the places he'd ever gone to work before—the oil rigs here, out to Alberta, some places in Toronto and Winnipeg—but he hadn't gone back to any of them.

MARY
Does the fact that the police are still looking for Dermot give you

some hope that he may yet be found? I know at CBC we've covered a few stories where a person who had lost all hope took up life as a homeless person for some years but then was discovered by friends or family and eventually found a better life again.

REET

I don't know, Mary. Here in Newfoundland, there's different people have gone missing in the past while, and after they've been gone for a few months they either turn up dead or never turn up at all. There was that man always played accordion for years along Water Street in St John's just disappeared six months ago and his remains were found outside of Moncton only last week. Before that, a fella at Harbour Grace stepped out of his house one evening to get a few sticks of firewood from his own woodshed and was never seen again. And Dermot's not the first one to disappear from the Harbour. There was young Jimmy Semple before him, went off with his girlfriend to Toronto and then just vanished. One day seven years ago, he left the apartment and just disappeared without a trace.

> *Mary is visibly startled and troubled at the mention of Jimmy Semple.*

MARY

But Jimmy Semple was from St John's, not from Halloran Harbour.

REET

Well, he was, and he was not. My niece Angie married Roland Semple after he came out here, doing work on the weather station. She died giving birth to Jimmy and Roly just fell apart, left the Harbour and never came back. Me and my sister Bea raised Jimmy; he was our little darling!

But Roly got his life back together after a while, married a lovely woman and they sent for Jimmy to come live with them in St John's. So, off he went to his own good home in the city when he was five years old. He never came back either. My, how we missed our little Jimmy! And we all felt the loss again when we heard he'd disappeared.

What do you think, Mary? I expect you've covered a lot of news stories about people disappearing. What happens to these people who go missing and never come home?

Mary loses the smooth interviewer manner and voice, her attitude altered by some inner turmoil.

MARY
Well, I suppose there must be accidents that no one sees, and the victims just never are found, and of course there's a criminal world out there, with drugs and such, that people sometimes get too close to whether they mean to or not.

REET
But how can it be, Mary? A man tells his wife he's going out to fetch some firewood from the shed and she never sees him again, in some little village out around the bay where everyone knows everyone. How does a Jimmy Semple just walk out of his apartment one day and disappear? Are there so many criminals all around us, preying on people? Are there so many desperate souls just want to disappear forever?

Short pause.

Mary
(with barely-controlled vehemence)
Sometimes it's only justice, Reet. Sometimes…those missing people

150

just get...what they deserve!

Reet looks at Mary with surprise and alarm.
Mary's expression changes slowly from stern to be-wildered, to full-on tears. When Mary clearly is on the way to tears, Reet reaches across the table and turns off the voice re-corder Short pause. Mary sobs.
Reet takes Mary's hands in her own and Mary bursts into louder tears.

REET
Mary, dear! Tell me, what is it? What have I said?

MARY
(through her tears)
I killed Jimmy Semple, Reet! He didn't disappear. He beat me and hurt me, and I killed him.

Short pause.

MARY
I killed your baby, Reet!

Short pause.

MARY
But you've got some secrets too, Reet. You're not living in this cold harsh place just because you want to, like you let on. There's something else is keeping you here.

Mary continues to sob uncontrollably.

Reet rises and fetches from a shelf a 1/3 full bottle of rum. She pours a generous portion in each of their teacups, caps the bottle, and sets it on the table. She hands a cup to Mary, who takes it mechanically.

Reet takes a big swallow from the other cup. Mary hesitates, then takes a similarly large drink. She is getting her tears under control.

Reet sits.

REET
(with calm reserve)
Tell me, Mary.

MARY
I loved him, Reet. I loved Jimmy, right from high school. He was big and handsome and everyone's favourite, and he chose me out of the crowd. He was fun and mad for sex and lovely, and he went with me to Toronto when I got into journalism at Ryerson. Jimmy wasn't much for school, but he got different jobs and helped pay the rent.

But then he changed, wasn't so nice, wanted stuff in bed I didn't want to do, but he insisted. But I was still crazy about him. I wanted to do whatever he asked, to keep him happy; I was terrified of the thought he might leave me.

Short pause. Reet drains her teacup, and Mary follows suit.

REET
The trouble with men has always been that they're in the way of being pigs, and the trouble with women has always been that we can't help but love those pigs.

MARY

He got violent, Reet. He was drinking and smoking dope and maybe other stuff that he never did before, and he wanted me to do it too. He pushed me around, he slapped me a lot and sometimes he half strangled me. He wanted me to sleep with some of his friends, and I did it for him, but then I saw they were paying him for it.

One night he told me he had to make more money and that I had to go to a hotel room he'd rented and have sex with two or three different guys he'd arranged with.

That's when my balloon burst. I told him I'd do no such thing and that he'd better pack his bags right now and get out.

REET
(not a question)
And then he tried to kill you.

MARY
(in tears again)
He did, Reet. He punched me wherever he could and cornered me in the kitchen with a wine bottle, ready to smash it over my head. There was a wee sharp knife on the counter, and when he raised that bottle, I grabbed it and stuck it straight into his heart...straight into that big soft warm chest I used to curl up against, feeling so loved and happy.

Mary cries, and after a time regains a bit of composure.

REET
No one ever found Jimmy. What did you do with him?

MARY

I was paralyzed, Reet. I was stunned. I stood there for a lifetime, looking at him sprawled on the floor where he'd just sunk down and died. I felt every emotion there is to feel, all mixed up and contrary.

Finally, I sank down onto the floor, too, and I reached for that bottle of wine was meant to kill me. I drank it all, one little sip at a time, and by the time I was done, I knew there was no one to call for help and nothing right or wrong or clever or sensible to do.

There was a big construction dumpster for roof repair on the street, three floors straight down from our window. I hauled and heaved Jimmy out that window and threw after him everything in the apartment that was his. Then I went to bed and waited for the police to come.

It was freezing cold and snowing hard that night. I lay there for about a day and a half, but no one ever came by to ask about Jimmy.

After a week or two his parents, Roly and Pam, started calling me because they couldn't get him on the phone. I told them he'd left me. A while later, they reported him missing.

> *Pause, maybe 15 seconds.*
> *Reet reaches for the rum bottle and pours another hefty dose into their teacups. She holds Mary's teacup up to her until she takes it, then takes up her own. They both drink, Reet slowly and fully, Mary hesitantly and lightly.*

REET

This rum is the last drink Dermot ever took, Mary.

MARY

What do you mean?

REET

I've been telling lies, Mary, same as you. Dermot never disappeared. I killed him. I killed him right here in this cellar. You're sitting on top of what's left of him.

Mary looks around her, including at the floor, partly confused and partly horrified. Then she looks Reet deeply in the eyes. Then, more calmly, she reaches for her teacup and takes a substantial sip.

MARY

Tell me, Reet.

Reet takes a drink, sets down her cup.

REET

Dermot was a fine man, and a fine father, but the world turned on him and broke him. He turned sad and then he turned desperate and then he turned angry. He'd never been a man to drink but he turned to it then.

Twenty-five years ago, he hit me for the first time and straight away he left the Harbour to look for work, kind of to say he was sorry. But each time he came back, it was a little worse.

It was only me he beat up at first, and I got Dora out of here before he ever hurt her. But he turned me black and blue, and he started picking fights with others and scaring young girls.

The whole Harbour knew how dangerous he'd become. It had to end.

MARY

What did you do?

REET
I drew a line in the sand. I moved into this cellar and told him
never to come in here after me, but I knew that sooner or later he
would come. He needed to end his misery and he didn't much see a
difference between killing himself and killing me. One day he'd
come for me down that ladder, with a knife or a crowbar or an axe
or something, and it would be me or him.

MARY
When did he come?

REET
In February a year and a half ago, in the dark of night. He shouted
down at me, "Reet, I'm comin' down." And I yelled back that if he
tried to come down, I'd kill him.
   Down he came, holding the ladder and that rum bottle with one
hand and his splitting axe in the other.
   As he came down, I stuck him all the way through the back with
that fish fork, and when he fell to the floor, I stuck him again. He
never moved after that.

MARY
And you buried him...here?

REET
Yes, my dear. There were six big bags of old fish salt down here
when I set this cellar up for living, and I just kept them here, with a
shovel beside them.

> *Pause, maybe 10 seconds.*
>   *Mary empties here teacup in one swallow. She resettles her-*
> *self in her chair, and looks up at Reet with an inviting smile.*

*She re-positions the microphone and turns the voice recorder
on again.*

MARY
Reet, it seems you kind of set this cellar up like your own version
of a "man-cave," a refuge where you could do your own thing. But
then, with Dermot gone, you've come to feel more comfortable just
living here than in the old house you once shared. Will you make
this your home from now on?

REET
(back in her role as interviewee)
No, my dear, I will not. It's been lovely, but it's been lonely, too.
Dora and Armand are after building a whole apartment for me off
the back of their house in Halifax, and the grandkids are waiting.
I'll be heading there in a few days time.

MARY
And how do you think the vote on resettlement will go? It's only
two days away, isn't it?

REET
Everyone in the Harbour knows how the vote will go. There's not a
person here would vote against it if they thought their vote would
change the outcome. For all the talk, no one is going to stay. We all
know we have to move on.

MARY
What will happen to your house, and to this "woman-cave"?

Reet chuckles.

REET
Well, this woman is going to leave her cave for sure. The houses likely will get torn down for the lumber; there won't be anything left inside them.

There's lots of other cellars like this one around the Harbour and some people figure they'll be a danger to the public in the future, especially to tourists or whoever might visit the Harbour down the road and maybe fall into them. They're all to be filled in.

My nephew with his backhoe will be a busy man for a few weeks. I asked him to do my cellar the day before I leave, so I can stay with it until its last day.

MARY
Well, Reet, it has been lovely talking with you.
(To her imaginary listeners)
I have been speaking with Mrs. Rita Crocker, the lady who became notorious recently for living for nearly four years in a root cellar in the village of Halloran Harbour. Thank you for sharing your story with us, Reet, and we wish you all the best on your next adventures.

> *Mary switches off the voice recorder, takes a deep breath and is no longer the professional reporter. She picks up the recorder.*

MARY
Will I take this back to my producers, Reet? I can lose it easy enough; I can just drop it overboard on the boat this evening.

REET
You take that back with you, Mary. You just do your job. There's no hurt or shame has got into that machine.

Mary looks at the recorder, then busily packs it and the microphone in her briefcase. She looks at her wristwatch.

MARY
I'd best be on my way. Joey Frampton said he'd have to leave by 4 o'clock to be sure of fair weather and a safe trip back here after he drops me off.

> *Mary stands, takes off her gloves.*
> *Reet stands. Mary hands her the gloves.*
> *They look at each other, then fall into an intense embrace.*

MARY
We won't ever tell anyone will we?

REET
There's no one left to tell, Mary, now that we've told ourselves.

> *They stand back from their embrace, holding each others' arms, hands to elbows.*

MARY
I get to Halifax a lot in my work, Reet. Do you think I could visit you sometime, when I'm there?

REET
Don't you even think of staying in a hotel there again, Mary. Promise me you'll stay with me, every time. I'll be waiting for you, just like my grandkids are waiting for me.

> *They embrace again, deeply but briefly. Then Mary quickly goes up the ladder, stands on the ground beside the compan-*

ionway for a moment, takes a deep breath, and EXITS.

Reet watches her go up the ladder, stares up after her as she departs, then turns back into her cellar room. She picks up her fiddle, and sits in her chair. She pauses in thought for another moment, then begins to play the same tune again.

FADE TO BLACK.
MUSIC OUT.

Ted and Alec Leighton

Notes

These stories are of events and people, real, remembered and imagined. The stories from Nova Scotia in the 1920s and1930s were
written by Alexander Leighton (1908-2007) mostly in the 1990s,
from his memories across the intervening decades of his personal
friends, acquaintances and heroes, called by their real names as
best he could remember them.

Ted Leighton extracted the stories posthumously from his
father's unpublished writing, and organized, edited and provided
background to them for this volume.

'The Crossing' and the story of Curt Rice were taken from an interview of Alexander Leighton recorded by Harold and Diane
Clapp in their home in Smiths Cove, Nova Scotia in 2003.

The history lesson from Bob Cossett was taken directly from the
written record of the interview described in that chapter.

Ted Leighton wrote the story of Louie Penny, based on his parti-
cipation in the described adventure at about age 6. He also wrote
the stories of Kate Daily and John McGuire, 'The Emerald Isle' and
'The Immigrant's Tale'.

Maggie Morine and Reet Crocker are fictional characters repres-
entative of real people who inspired Ted Leighton to write their
stories.

The Magic Show

In the first paragraph, reference is made to *Bert and I*, and related stories. Print, audio and electronic book versions of these stories are available from various commercial sources.

The print edition of *Bert and I: and Other Stories from Down East*, 2nd Edition, by Marshall Dodge and Robert Bryan, is published by Down East Books.

Readers wishing to know more about Bill and Danny, William Main Doerflinger (1910–2000) and Daniel Pratt Mannix IV (1911-1997), will find biographical profiles on line through Wikipedia and other sites. Two relevant books are:

> *Shantymen and Shantyboys: Songs of the Sailor and Lumberman* by William Doerflinger. New York: MacMillan, 1951.
> *Step Right Up* by Daniel Mannix, New York: Harper & Brothers, 1951.

Boudica

The scientific publications arising from Alec Leighton's study of beavers at Loud Lake in 1931 are:

> Leighton, A. H. 1932. Notes on the beaver's individuality and mental characteristics. *Journal of Mammalogy*. Vol. 13, pages 117-126.
> Leighton, A. H. 1933. Notes on the relations of beavers to one another and to the muskrat. *Journal of Mammalogy*. Vol.14, pages 27-35.

The Crossing

Alec Leighton's cousin and companion on this 1927 adventure was Will (William James) Leighton (1908-2001) from County Down in Ireland. He entered the Embassy Theatre School of Acting in London in 1934 and, from a base in London, was active on stage, television and screen for 50 years. More detail can be found on line at www.ulsteractors.com/l/ .

John McGuire

The Lord of the Rings, by J. R. R. Tolkien, consists of three books: *The Fellowship of the Ring* (published July 1954), *The Two Towers* (November 1954) and *The Return of the King* (October 1955). The character Sam Gamgee appears in all three.

Ted and Alec Leighton

Acknowledgements

Eva McCauley made the ten original drawings that so wonderfully illustrate this book; Past to Present Photos of Lequille, Nova Scotia digitized them; and Rebekah Wetmore of Moose House Publications did the final work to prepare them for printing.

Andrew Wetmore, editor at Moose House, envisioned and encouraged the co-authorship of this book, and his expert editing brought improvements to every chapter. He and Lenny Shirose assisted in creating the regional maps.

Harold and Diane Clapp contributed a recorded interview with A. H. Leighton and their own memories of conversations with him.

Conversations with Niel Brennan, Félix Comeau and Frank Meuse provided context for several stories.

Ted and Alec Leighton

About the authors

Alec (Alexander) Hamilton Leighton MD was a research psychiatrist who, with his psychiatrist wife, Dorothea Leighton, pioneered the study of levels and distributions of mental illness in human populations and of medical anthropology. In 1948, they designed and initiated a long-term study of psychiatric epidemiology in Digby County Nova Scotia, the *Stirling County Study*, which continued for several decades.

During World War II, Alec Leighton served in a US Naval Intelligence unit focused on Japan, which advised strongly against deployment there of nuclear weapons.

He had academic appointments at Cornell University, Harvard University and Dalhousie University. He was especially proud of his election to membership in the American Philosophical Society and of being granted, based on knowledge and competence, a license as a back-county guide in the forests of Nova Scotia.

Notable publications include:

The Governing of Men: General Principles and Recommendations Based on Experience at a Japanese Relocation Camp, Princeton: Princeton University Press, 1945.

Human Relations in a Changing World: Observations on the Use of the Social Sciences, New York: E. P. Dutton, 1949.

My Name is Legion: Foundations for a Theory of Man in Relation to Culture, The Stirling County Study of Psychiatric Disorder and Sociocultural Environment, Volume I, New York: Basic Books,

1959.

People of Cove and Woodlot: Communities from the Viewpoint of Social Psychiatry. The Stirling County Study of Psychiatric Disorder and Sociocultural Environment, Volume II, New York: Basic Books, 1960.

The Character of Danger: Psychiatric Symptoms in Selected Communities. The Stirling County Study of Psychiatric Disorder and Sociocultural Environment, Volume III, New York: Basic Books, 1963.

'Poverty and social change', *Scientific American,* Vol. 212, 1965, pp. 21-24.

Come Near (a novel), New York: W. W. Norton, 1971.

A. H. Leighton, E. A. Mason, J. C. Kern and F. A. Leighton, 'Moving pictures as an aid in community development', *Human Organization* Vol. 31, 1972, pp. 11-21.

Caring for Mentally Ill People: Psychological and Social Barriers in Historical Context, New York: Cambridge University Press, 1982.

A full collection of professional and personal papers, letters, photographs and much else from Alexander Leighton and his forebears is archived and indexed in the Dalhousie University Archives in Halifax, Canada.

Ted (Frederick) Leighton O.C. is professor emeritus at the University of Saskatchewan and professeur associé at Université Sainte-Anne. From 1984 to 2015, he was a professor of veterinary pathology at the Western College of Veterinary Medicine and was the founding director of the Canadian Wildlife Health Cooperative.

Since retiring from academic science, he has focused on creative writing and local nature conservation projects.

He lives in Bear River, Nova Scotia with his partner, the artist Eva McCauley.

Notable publications include:

A Ring of Justice (a novel), Perotte, NS: Moose House Publications, 2022.

Knowers and Lovers (a novel), Perotte, NS: Moose House Publications, 2024.

'So many dead herring: Citizen scientists tackle a marine mystery in southwestern Nova Scotia', *Rural Delivery*, January-February 2018, pp. 37-39.

F. A. Leighton, P. A. Leighton, S. Wood, T. Kuiken, 'Revenge of the Trees: Environmental Determinants and Population Effects of Infectious Disease Outbreaks on A Breeding Colony of Double-Crested Cormorants (*Phalacrocorax Auritus*) Over a Period of 21 Years'. *Journal of Wildlife Diseases, 2021,* Vol. 57, pp. 773–783.

A. H. Leighton, E. A. Mason, J. C. Kern and F. A. Leighton, 'Moving pictures as an aid in community development'. *Human Organization*, 1972, Vol. 31, pp. 11-21.

Ted and Alec Leighton

About the artist

Eva McCauley MFA is a painter and printmaker whose images of sky, water and shifting landscapes merge abstraction with figuration, and explore the ever-changing conditions of people and their environments. In her most recent landscape paintings she is increasingly concerned with the climate crisis, particularly its effect on ocean environments.

She studied visual art at the Ontario College of Art and Design, the University of Guelph and the University of Waterloo, and taught visual art at the University of Waterloo for 18 years. She has exhibited nationally and internationally, and her work is in many public and private collections. Most recently the UNB Art Centre Permanent Collection and the Nova Scotia Art Bank (2022) have acquired her paintings. Eva has received numerous grants and awards, including a Nova Scotia Creation Grant.

Her work can be viewed at evamccauley.com, and she is represented by the Agora Gallery in Stratford, Ontario: agoragallery.ca.

She lives and works in Bear River, Nova Scotia.